LITERARY LIVES

EDITED BY

W. ROBERTSON NICOLL

———

ERNEST RENAN

An immense river of oblivion sweeps us onward into a gulf without a name. O abyss, thou art the only God! The tears of all peoples are tears indeed; the dreams of all wise men have in them a parcel of the truth. All here below is but symbol and dream. The gods pass away like men; it would not be well did they last forever. The faith which we have held ought never to be a chain. We have done our duty by it when we have carefully wrapped it round in the purple shroud wherein the dead gods sleep.

My life has been such as I desired, such as I conceived to be the best. Had I to live it over again, I should make very little change. On the other hand, I am not much afraid of the future. I shall have my biography and my legend.

—Ernest Renan.

Ernest Renan.
From a painting by Henry Scheffer, 1860
Mme. Psichari's Collection

ERNEST RENAN

BY

WILLIAM BARRY, D.D.

ILLUSTRATED

NEW YORK
CHARLES SCRIBNER'S SONS
1905

Copyright, 1905, by
CHARLES SCRIBNER'S SONS

Published, April, 1905

TROW DIRECTORY
PRINTING AND BOOKBINDING COMPANY
NEW YORK

CONTENTS

CHAPTER VII

CHAPTER VIII

SOME LEADING DATES

ERNEST RENAN

Born at Tréguier	1823
Student in Paris	1838–1845
Leaves St. Sulpice	1845
Mission to Italy	1849
Succeeds Augustin Thierry	1856
Mission to Syria	1860
Chair of Hebrew	1861
Publishes *Life of Jesus*	1863
Travels in Asia Minor and Greece	1865
St. Paul published	1869
Resumes Chair of Hebrew	1870
Antichrist published	1873
Elected to French Academy	1879
Reminiscences of Youth	1883
Philosophic Dramas	1886
History of Israel	1888
Dies	1892
Monument at Tréguier	1903

LIST OF ILLUSTRATIONS

The publishers wish to acknowledge their indebtedness to Madame Psichari and M. Armand-Dayot for kind permission to include some of the illustrations.

CHAPTER I

THE BRETON PEASANT

BRITTANY, the green and gray land where, according to legend, Merlin the enchanter lies in a magic sleep under the white thorn near Paimpol—this rock-bound, sea-beaten coast, famous for its storms and its disasters—has given birth to men who, while in language they were French or Latin, kept the Celtic heart, and charmed the world with Celtic eloquence. In the early Middle Ages, Abelard, born at Palais near Nantes in 1079, lived out his romance amid the battle-cries that ushered in, on the site of the Latin Quarter at Paris, a great secular period, the term of which none may foresee. Abelard is the first of modern thinkers, pointing the way through scholastic mazes to Renaissance and Revolution. He is Yea and Nay, " Sic et non," alive to both sides of an argument, subtle, proud, self-determined, unhappy, and he stores up an inheritance which others turn to better account. He is the most illustrious of Bretons, yet a rebel against Church authority, a strange complex creature, a lover and a penitent, condemned yet devout. He has left a name over which disputes never have ceased, nor will cease. We admire, distrust, and pity Abelard. But singular as he remains in his greatness, he has had no successor more closely akin to him than Ernest Renan.

Passing over seven hundred years we come to the melancholy and splendid Chateaubriand, who first saw the light at St. Malo, created in his *René* the latest type of Hamlet, which Byron reproduced in *Childe Harold,* and dazzled the opening nineteenth century with a *Genius of Christianity,* framed in rhetoric of a high order but in somewhat fading colors. To him we may oppose the figure of Lamennais, priest, republican, apostate, revolutionary, whose tragic fortunes, gleams of inspiration, and unmanageable temper, set him apart from friends and foes, and whose ideas have won their triumphs while he rests at Père la Chaise in an unknown grave. Had Lamennais not fallen away from Rome, he would have shared with Newman the foremost honors among Churchmen of his day. But, like Abelard, he went down in a crusade on behalf of the fresh thought which was effacing ancient landmarks, confusing minds, and troubling Israel.

Those who are acquainted with no more than

the outlines of Renan's life, will yet be feeling, in what has just been said, how much he owes to Brittany; how he recalls Abelard by his perpetual balancing of Yea and Nay; how he manipulates a style as creative as Chateaubriand's, though less brilliant and, in its shades, more exquisite; how he is, like Lamennais, " un prêtre manqué "; and how striking is the parallel which may be drawn by way of contrast between himself and Newman.

In all these dramas, reaching over hundreds of years, the protagonist, ever in the arena, is the Catholic Church. Loved or hated, that Church, as if it were the Fate in old Greek stories, furnishes the matter, interposes at a given moment, and unbinds the issue which at last it decides. What interest can equal this, whether we seek pathos or sublime effects, or the complication of moods and action, or the human touch, transfiguring to lucid and beautiful imagery motives, conceptions, resolves, otherwise hidden from our eyes? From Abelard, dying in 1142, down to Renan, whose funeral date is 1892, we reckon seven hundred and fifty years, during which the world's debate has gone on without intermission; and philosophy, science, dogma, have ever met in conflict, while ever aiming at friendship. Who can pretend to be impartial, that is to say, coldly indifferent, when he looks on these things? Certainly not the present writer. Nevertheless, in describing that career which Renan did not hesitate to qualify as his " charming promenade through the nineteenth century," I hope not to indulge in caricature, and I shall spare invective. The tale may often be told in its hero's own words, choice and discreetly sarcastic; sometimes, but rarely, touching; and if we do not deny ourselves the grain of salt which is to season his *Dichtung und Wahrheit,* we have his leave in the preface to the *Reminiscences,* where he warns us frankly that no man is ever quite candid about himself.

Ernest Renan was born at Tréguier, on February 27, 1823. Tréguier is an old decaying town, looking out toward the broad English Channel from its high hill, crowned with a soaring Gothic cathedral of the fourteenth century; a town of long silent streets bordered with convent walls over which, in summer, the foliage hangs abundantly. Many churches and chapels, each with its legend, give the place, which was long a bishop's See, the air, says Renan, of Benares and Jagatnata. Religion has ever been to the Bretons home and country; as heathen they believed in Fairyland; when they were made Christian, they worshipped their innumerable saints. Tréguier had its chapel of Saint Yves, the father of orphans, to whom Renan's widowed mother dedicated her child; it had a holy well near Notre Dame du Tromeur; and a Madonna in painted wood to which the people came on pilgrimage. These memories and customs lasted on, all through the Terror, the wars of Napoleon, the Bourbon Restoration. Such dates were accidents in the life of Tréguier, which went on dreaming of the fifth century, when its first inhabitants passed over sea from Wales. Its patron was St. Tudwal, whom it inserted in the list of Popes; was not his real name Pabu Tual? The Cathedral marked another stage. This Breton bishopric was made subject to Tours, not willingly, for it cherished its immemorial freedom. Then, in the seventeenth century, the bishop's house and the convents were founded. At the Revolution the last bishop fled to England. Napoleon suppressed the See: But when the Bourbons came back, an ecclesiastical school was set up in the old seminary; the convents flourished again; and in this atmosphere, pious and mediæval, but more profoundly Celtic, Renan drew his first breath.

Looking back over the past at Athens in 1865, when the *Life of Jesus* had brought him a reputation beyond all he could ever have anticipated, he delights to dwell on his descent from sailors and adventurers in the misty seas of the West. The good old clan which came from Cardigan to Goëlo, and still abounds there, was called after St. Renan or Ronan, a very singular hermit, equally obstinate alive or dead. But he was also proud of his mother's Gascon wit and humor, as accounting for his own. This admirable woman was a small bright figure, speaking Breton excellently well, and her children—an elder son, Alain, her daughter Henriette, and Ernest—learned it in their young days. All Madame Renan's influence made for piety and a loyal attachment to the House of France; by no means to Louis Philippe, whom she and her friends despised as a traitor that had filched the crown and put it in his pocket. Her kindred were of the middle class, moderately well to do, and Ernest paid them visits in Lannion, which struck him as a very worldly and frivolous place, compared with meditative Tréguier. But on the father's side traditions and principles were altogether different, and in fact revolutionary.

Ernest was only five when that father's dead body was found on the sands of Erquy, in August, 1828, under circumstances that pointed to suicide. A month earlier the boat of which he was master had come into port at Tréguier without him. Dreamy and never sanguine, he could make nothing of business, any more than the other Renans, all of whom, said their most famous descendant gayly, were as poor as Job, except one, who accumulated a fortune and got a bad name by trading in negroes. But Captain Renan had seen service under Villaret Joyeuse; he had fallen into the hands of the English and been compelled to work several years " sur les pontons," an indefinite phrase, which may signify hard labor at Portsmouth or some naval station. Ernest's grandfather, too, was an ardent patriot; his uncles on that side were even Jacobins. But the patriot grandfather would not buy any of the so-called " national estates," the proceeds of a ruthless confiscation, which were put up for sale in the open market.

Such conduct implies a rare degree of generosity. Whether Catholics or Republicans, his kindred were teaching the lad to sacrifice worldly advantages for the sake of a cause, be it the " Kingdom of God " or the " principles of humanity." That he learned the lesson is undoubted; we cannot, however, follow his course through life without observing in him a sense of the practical and a sagacity in making the most of his opportunities, which he can hardly have derived from his Breton ancestors.

His training was to be wholly clerical. In the long silent streets this ugly little lad, square built, with a head too large for his frail body, and with grave dreamy eyes which took in more than they expressed, went to and fro, between the quaint old house where he was born and the college where he learned his lessons. As a child he was very delicate. His life had hung on a thread, and he tells how the witch-wife Gode—that is to say, Kate —had taken one of his little shirts when he was two months old, gone down to the "sacred spring," and conjured with it by flinging it out on the waters. If it sank, he would soon die; if it floated, he was saved. She came back triumph-ant. "He means to live! He means to live!" she cried in ecstasy. The white garment had spread its arms and flown over the wavelets. "From that hour," says Renan, smiling, "I was a favorite with the fairies, and I loved them in turn." We Celts, he goes on to observe, shall never build the Parthenon, we have no marble; but we know how to lay hold of the heart and the soul; we dip our hands into the very inmost of man, and we draw them forth, as did the witches in *Macbeth,* full of the secrets of infinitude. The old religion, which in the twelfth century came under Norman and Mediæval-Roman usages, as in the seventeenth it was guided by the Jesuits, had never lost its more primitive color among the Bretons.

These things gave to the incomparable child of genius a rich, dim background whereon to embroider his early ambitions and phantasies, and afterward the whole world, Parisian, Greek, Oriental, which he conquered in thought and travelling. Very poor, cut off apparently from the best of education, he gained in secluded Tréguier the one thing which our schools cannot yield—a perfect detachment from " das Gemeine was uns alle bändigt." That is ever the condition of poetry and the ideal. In a crowd what room is there for distinction? But Ernest Renan kept aloof at all times from the crowd, even when as a too indulgent sceptic in his last days he flattered many a national weakness.

The Church brought him up. Her serious and disinterested clergy—M. Pasco, M. Duchêne, M. Auffret, and others whom he names affectionately —taught him all they knew. They were scarcely advanced beyond the year 1630 in their methods; to their feeling no religious verse had been written since the younger Racine laid down his pen. They could not bear Lamartine's hymns and elegies, though he too had been moulded by clerics. Victor Hugo was to them unknown, as much as the French of Paris to Chaucer's Prioress in Stratford-atte-Bowe. History they learned in Rollin. On verse-making they looked as a dangerous excitement, not to be encouraged. Hence Renan, like some other great masters of prose—Balzac,

George Sand, Pierre Loti—could not manage the French Alexandrine couplet, whereby the world has had no loss that we need lament. Natural science was neglected; yet we should bear in mind that other ecclesiastics outside Tréguier had taken an honorable share in the development of physics and biology. But these good Bretons taught mathematics well, and Renan felt a passionate drawing to that discipline, as Newman also did. His comrade, Guyomar, kept pace with him in all his lessons; and the two boys chalked up problems as they went home, on the great closed gates of the old mansions which they passed by.

Renan's father had left nothing but debts. His brave mother found it hard to get food and fuel in the winter. His clothes were often patched, his shoes clouted. For the kindest things in life he was indebted to his sister Henriette, twelve years older than himself—the real good fairy whose plain features hid an exquisite soul, and whose devotion to him knew no bounds. Yet he does not ascribe even to his beloved nurse and playmate the best that was in him. It is of the clergy at Tréguier that he writes: "They were my first spiritual teachers, and I owe to them whatever of good there may be in me. . . . I have had since masters more brilliant and sagacious; I have never had any more venerable; and that accounts for my frequent differences with some of my friends. I have had the happiness of knowing absolute virtue; I understand what faith is. . . . I feel that my life is always controlled by a faith which I possess no longer."

He calls that old time at college a " precious experience," though he read into it afterward " saintly illusions " and held it to be a divine deception. He became, as it were, the Orpheus of a lost Eurydice, the white seamew flying round about the ruined church of Saint Michael, which had been struck by lightning, and which the bird strives to enter, while the peasant that goes by murmurs on seeing it, " That is the soul of a priest who wants to say Mass." In vain for him to begin, " I will go unto the altar of God "; there is no server who may reply, " Unto God that giveth joy to my youth." Pretty enough, and true, and sad! Yet still more astonishing that Renan, in his thrice-fortunate old age, felt these regrets thus keenly.

Soldier or sailor, as his father was, he could not be. His shy reserve, his want of physical vigor, his growing thoughtfulness, and, above all, his absorption in books, predestined him for the sanctuary. He spent delightful hours in the Cathedral; he loved to fancy himself a priest. Nevertheless, Renan was neither then nor afterward exactly devout. A pattern scholar, he took prizes and kept the top of his form. But he came late to Mass; he offered none of those tokens by which the youthful saint is recognizable. His vocation —a solemn word among Catholics, who liken every true priest to the young Samuel—grew out of his love for learning. He did not look forward to missionary or parochial duties; and when he lightly sketches what his career might have been in the diocese of St. Brieuc, it is as a professor, a vicar-general, and a canon lawyer that he sees himself enjoying an excellent reputation.

From the first he wanted to know all things. But he was very innocent. The other boys called him "Mademoiselle," and played tricks on him. The girls, he says, found him "quiet and reasonable." He tells the story of one, Noemi, for whom he had a liking, which naturally faded away as he turned toward his predestined novitiate. He was learning the classics—a bad sign his uncle Renan, the watchmaker, thought it, and warned him not to become what La Fontaine called in the fable an "ass, burdened with Latin." For this prototype of M. Homais, the bourgeois Voltairian whom we have all laughed over in *Madame Bovary,* desired Ernest to succeed him at the shop. That, indeed, might have come to pass, had not the good fairy, Henriette, written from Paris in a decisive moment, which brought in its wake the most astonishing change of fortune.

Henriette, too, was highly endowed. She had learned Latin from an old Ursuline nun; but her special gift was teaching, and her French in time acquired a purity, strength, and clearness which would have charmed the *grand siècle*. Her character was cast on antique lines. Resolved to pay her father's debts, she had gone up to Paris in 1835, and endured the solitary griefs and harsh treatment of a governess in fashionable schools. But she made friends, studied sixteen hours a day, and would not despair. At home she had refused an offer of marriage, honorable in itself, but which would have separated her from her family. Alain, it appears, was settled in Paris. Henriette spoke of her brother Ernest, who had taken all the first prizes in his school at Tréguier, to a zealous Catholic physician, M. Descuret; and he, in turn, brought the list of distinctions (a striking document which is still in existence) under the notice of M. Dupanloup.

That celebrated man had achieved fame by securing the reconciliation to the Church—or, as it was termed, the repentance—on his death-bed, of M. le Prince de Talleyrand, formerly Bishop of Autun. As a reward, M. Dupanloup was set over the junior seminary, called St. Nicolas du

Chardonnet, in the Rue St. Victor at Paris, which he speedily raised to the first rank in point of numbers and renown. His cry was " Give me scholars "; rich or poor, it did not matter; he asked only for talent which he might educate. This Breton peasant's unusual record won his favor immediately. Dupanloup offered him on behalf of M. de Quélen, the archbishop, a clerical scholarship, tenable until Ernest should be twenty-five, on condition that it was accepted without delay. Henriette's letter, dated August 31, 1838, told the good news in fervent accents. Her brother must pack up at once, catch the diligence at Guingamp, borrow the necessary funds in her name from his uncle Forestier, and be in Paris on Wednesday evening or Thursday morning. " Tell mother that her boy's future is decided," Henriette wrote exultingly.

Far more, indeed, was at stake than she or anyone could imagine. This awkward, shy lad, a rustic in manners, poor and proud, was destined to become the supreme French writer of his century. He would not be a priest, but an artist of the Renaissance, exercising in all directions an influence which no other man has wielded. The Church was giving every advantage to a son who would turn out her resolute enemy, marked forever in the legend of his day as having attempted to rewrite the Gospel in secular and dilettante colors. It was the strangest of dramatic sequences in the nineteenth century which M. Dupanloup had, after this surprising fashion, inaugurated.

The lad, now in his sixteenth year, was staying at a place near Tréguier, when a messenger brought the happy news. Renan never forgot his walk home across country, under the setting sun, while village sent on to village the chimes of the Angelus, a symbol of that tranquil faith and life from which he was turning to plunge into our modern world. On September 7, 1838, he arrived in Paris; next day the kindly physician who had procured his scholarship took him to St. Nicolas, and on the day after begins his " correspondence while at the seminary," by means of which we may fill up and now and then rectify the memories long afterward written down at Ischia of Renan's critical period.

Those seven years which followed gave tone and meaning to his whole existence. They ran parallel, we must remember, to a movement at Oxford precisely the reverse of that whereby this lonely French student, sacrificing tradition to what he deemed scientific reason, was to exchange the Catholic creed for a Pantheism as vague as it was fascinating. Newman ended his seven years of argument and agony by submitting to the ancient

Church. Renan, twenty-two years his junior, in contact with a literature and philosophy—the German—which Herder, Kant, Hegel, displayed to his admiring view, but which Oxford had not begun to study, took up the problem at a stage further on. Church and Bible were thrown into the furnace of criticism. They came out wondrously transfigured, no longer supernatural, but mere episodes in a process to be measured by millions of years, during which the blind impulse that Schopenhauer defined as " the will to live " moved hither and thither in quest of satisfaction. Our interest in Renan will always be centred round this time. We know it intimately, thanks to his own letters and to Henriette's replies, every page on both sides remarkable for a choice of words which is enhanced by elevation of sentiment. Not in any degree picturesque, they are finely drawn, subtle, impassioned, at high moments pathetic. And through them all Madame Veuve Renan appears, a touching figure in her lonesome room at Tréguier—the pattern of a devout French mother who, in giving her son to God, had left her home desolate.

Mother and son felt it grievously. Ernest underwent, in his first months at St. Nicolas, a struggle with homesickness which told upon his lessons. It was a gay and lively house, pervaded by the energy of M. Dupanloup, who, though himself no deeply read classic, proved to be an " incomparable awakener." He spoke to the lads every evening in chapel, set them to strive one against another in themes and declamations, infected them with his own taste for rhetoric, and, on the whole, bore a singular likeness to Victor Cousin, at that time the most brilliant professor in Europe. But to a self-conscious little Breton, with manners no less timid than his appearance was ungainly, St. Nicolas seemed cold and sad. He was always writing home. One of his letters fell under Dupanloup's observation on a day when the places were to be read out. The young recruit was only fifth or sixth in French composition. " Ah," said Dupanloup, who loved his own mother fervently, despite his irregular birth, " if the subject had been that of a letter which I read this morning, Ernest Renan would have been first." From that time he took notice of the lad, and eclipsing his earlier masters by talents to which they could never have pretended, won his grateful and lasting attachment.

St. Nicolas, founded in the seventeenth century by Adrien de Bourdoise, had been, like the more celebrated St. Sulpice, a training-school for priests. It went down at the Revolution, and rose again in a very different form. M. de Quélen, Archbishop of Paris under Louis Philippe until 1840, was a prelate of the *ancien régime,* well descended, delicately feminine in his looks, who wore diamonds on great days, but was edifying after his manner. He believed in the tone of good society, and Dupanloup had that tone, as well as rarer gifts. Neither the Archbishop nor his *protégé* was much acquainted with divinity; the Fathers were to them venerable names, the Schoolmen not readable. And Dupanloup, gathering his two hundred pupils, lay and clerical, from all sides, while he made the wealthy pay for the destitute in a way that spared the most sensitive feelings, was intent on bringing out poets, literary men, and public speakers.

He set little store by erudition. But, observes Renan, the seminary has in France one advantage over the university: it does not burden the aspiring lad with classic dogmas and cast-iron programmes. None who are strangers to modern French life will understand how much is contained in this single sentence. M. Taine has denounced the Chinese inefficiency of a central Board, always behind the times, pedantic and absolute, which sacrifices original genius to red tape, and which creates not inventors or explorers but functionaries. At St. Nicolas the Romantic literature had fair play; Lamartine and Hugo were subjects of everlasting discussion. The Abbé Richard taught history on the newest principles; and his successor, though incapable as a master, read to his class extracts from Michelet, which intoxicated Renan, making him dream at night of that most musical prose.

Yet we remark two things, not without significance. The young scholar often failed in his French essay; and when writing home he kept to the simple, unaffected style which he had brought from Tréguier. His own explanation of our first point reveals the man; he " could not feel an interest in what he had not thought out for himself." The second is a mere but striking consequence of the first. Rhetoric seldom thinks for itself: it loves an argument ready made. It flourishes among Southerners; and though Renan boasted occasionally of his Gascon blood, he distrusted the loud, empty eloquence which, in Barère for example, could serve any cause at a moment's warning. For one who, in his finest pages, was hardly ever to be rhetorical, it was a sign of character that he refused to imitate Dupanloup. Not without meaning, also, does he observe, " At no time in my life was I obedient; I have been docile and submissive, but always to a spiritual principle, never to coercion." There speaks the Celt and the idealist.

He won no prizes at St. Nicolas for French or

Latin verse. But all knowledge came easy to him; the delicate Breton was never ill, and he showed not the least symptom, then or afterward, of that French ailment, *la névrose*. He had, in fact, a splendid constitution, which long resisted the want of exercise, mental vicissitudes, travels in Eastern climates, and the strain of work that paused for no consideration down to his dying day.

From his correspondence a pleasing yet often melancholy picture might be sketched of the poor clerical student and his widowed mother, while Henriette, earning her bread in Paris on such hard terms, is always the good angel of the story. She went to see him whenever it was allowed. Ernest is full of anxiety about the winter at home; wood is dear, and a cup of warm coffee, his mother's only gratification, costs money; but she ought to indulge herself. His own *bourse* did not provide him with clothes. There was trouble in getting an overcoat; and if Henriette were not there to mend his linen, he would have been put to shame, like many another famous youngster in the world's unfeeling annals. He had persuaded two of his comrades at home to follow his example and enter St. Nicolas. They arrived; but after a while Guyomar, his best friend, went back to Brittany, and died there of consumption; Liart could not live in the Parisian air, and he, too, gave up the

Tréguier.
Photo Paul Gruyer

chances of metropolitan success. Renan held out, won distinctions, was "crowned" in public five times on the same prize day, Henriette looking on, and already cherished in a stubborn silent fashion the resolve to make his way in Paris. Others might serve the Church elsewhere; he would devote himself to the saving of souls in that fierce Babylon. A sure instinct led him, even so young, toward the path of success and fame.

He was now seeing history as on an illuminated page. He heard the sound of Blanqui's insurrection, May 12, 1839; attended the Archbishop's requiem; listened to Lacordaire and Ravignan, the first of French pulpit orators; saw Napoleon's second funeral, on that bleak day in 1840; and found a place in Notre Dame, when the Comte de Paris was baptized, May 2, 1841. In the autumn of that year he went home, at the charge of Henriette, who was always finding money for every one's wants but her own. In January, 1842, he had left St. Nicolas, M. Dupanloup, the writing of Latin verse and French rhetoric. He was transferred to Issy, the country house where young ecclesiastics learned logic and metaphysics, took their minor orders, and were prepared to enter the "great seminary" of St. Sulpice.

An entirely new chapter was opening for him. Henriette, in January, 1841, had quitted her ungrateful task of teaching in Paris, and had accepted a position as governess in the household of Count Andrew Zamoyski, a Polish noble. Traversing the Black Forest in deep snow, she had met her new friends at Vienna and gone with them over the Carpathians, to their great house at Clemensoff, where she remained, except when the family was moving about, during the next ten years. Her sufferings and solitude had imprinted a stern character on the mind which was from early days disposed to severe thoughts. She was always, perhaps, inclined toward Jansenism. Little by little she had lost confidence in her Church altogether; but of that momentous change not a syllable had been whispered in her brother's hearing. If he was to go the same way, he must find it out for himself. So far, caught up in the literary tournaments of his class and in superficial studies, he had taken his vocation more or less for granted. He did not know his own mind. A few months of reading in philosophy were to teach him things he had never contemplated and to bring home to him the full extent of the sacrifice, or the consecration, demanded of a Catholic priest, once his engagement was taken. The decisive hours of his life were now to follow. What would be the result?

CHAPTER II

ECLIPSE OF FAITH

A LITTLE beyond the last houses of Vaugirard stands, in its own vast and agreeable park, the mansion of Issy, which serves as a preparatory school to St. Sulpice for clerics who are studying their " philosophy." The building is not remarkable, but its central feature is a pavilion, light and elegant in style, profusely painted inside with Renaissance emblems, which are due to Queen Margot, otherwise Marguerite de Valois, first wife of Henry IV, who resided here from 1606 till her death in 1616. After many changes the place was given in 1655 to M. Olier, who founded the Sulpician order. This eminent man has never been canonized. He displayed in his own person an austere piety, mingled with raptures and revelations on which he set no great value. The group to which he belonged had little in common with St. Francis de Sales or the Company of Jesus; but in many ways it reminds us of the early mediæval monks, especially by a certain spirit of quietness and freedom which left room for individuals to shape their own course.

The Sulpicians are not, strictly speaking, a religious order; they form a congregation of secular priests. That ill-natured historian, the Duc de Saint Simon, despised them as much as he hated the Jesuits; he mocks at their " extreme platitude," their cowardice, and their servile fear of the great Society in its palmy days. He could not understand the motives on which they shrank from the world's notice; why they dwelt in humble retirement, satisfied to train the clergy who were intrusted to them by the bishops from every part of France. But in Canada they acquired authority and large possessions, which they still retain; while in the United States they have won a reputation by their success in managing the diocesan seminaries.

Their fame is, however, collective; and their publications are, by preference, unsigned. Literature has always been to them the impersonal undertaking which it was to the Benedictines of St. Maur. They looked with apprehension upon the aspiring Dupanloup, whom their silence appeared to censure. It must, indeed, be admitted that from the mixed school of St. Nicolas, despite its attractions, not a candidate was gained for holy orders outside the clerical bourses. St. Sulpice received students from every French diocese; it brought them up on a system which had not changed since the days of Bossuet and Olier, and which was as unlike as it well could be to Dupanloup's literary forcing-house. In metaphysics St. Sulpice was Cartesian; in Christian evidences it would take no account of Chateaubriand or De Maistre; it became almost passionate in its opposition to Lamennais, whose apologetics frankly gave up the argument from reason to seek refuge in the "universal testimony" of mankind. But it would not have refused to join hands with Paley, Thomas Reid, and the moderate orthodox, to whom was owing the so-called philosophy of common sense.

The park at Issy, with its painted chapels and images of saints, had already witnessed a discussion of first principles inside that historic arbor in which Bossuet, Fénelon, and the Abbé Tronson drew up their thirty-four articles on "true and false Mysticism" in 1694. It contained several fine pieces of water, which froze in January on the high ground open toward the north. Long lines of hornbeam made in it pleasant alleys, under the shade of which young Renan passed his hours, reading, debating with his own mind, drinking deep draughts of philosophic doubt. He was not like Sainte Beuve, tormented by a thirst after the divine life; but his dawning instinct for art and letters enabled him to find satisfaction in the exercises of the chapel. No sooner did he grasp the import of logic, with its immediate application to problems that he had never before dreamed of, than his whole being underwent a crisis. He had hitherto believed in his teachers as if they were the oracles of God. Now he resolved, in accordance with the maxims of Descartes, to take nothing for certain that was not clear and evident to himself.

Writing to his mother, he describes the place in charming though not vivid colors. He was learning from *Télémaque* how to paint landscapes and persons by " moral touches "; for apart from this human aspect they left him unmoved. Turgenieff, the admirable Russian, whose power was of a different kind, has censured the indefinite outlines which he marked in Renan's autobiography. But we cannot complain that their disciple fails in sketching his Sulpician masters—M. Gosselin, the polite and learned superior of Issy, who became his spiritual director; M. Gottofrey, who taught metaphysics while utterly scorning them; and M. Pinault, professor of mathematics, who despised science altogether. M. Pinault led on a band of mystical scholars to high devotion; he was a sort of Catholic M. Littré, too original for the society into which he had passed from the University. A character yet more strange was Hanique, the lay hall-porter, saintly and simple, recognized as a light in things of the spirit, and consulted by the ardent youths who exalted holiness above knowledge.

Renan took his own way, as he did at all times. He was not a favorite with his companions. M. l'Abbé Cognat, who knew him well at the seminary, and others not unqualified to judge, have recognized his own somewhat too flattering portrait of the reserved and silent rustic—his manners had still much to gain—who would not follow M. Pinault's direction, nor lose faith in reason though it confounded him, and whose verdict on the professor of philosophy was the ironical but just remark that in metaphysics you cannot have a master.

His solitude was unbroken. For two years he never went into Paris. For months he did not stir beyond the park at Issy. Reading grew to be a devouring passion, which absorbed the hours he should have given to exercise. It was the freshman's year with him, full of excitement, unsettling and feverish like any other initiation into the realities of life. Young men commonly pass out of this green sickness to find themselves acquiescing in the beliefs which they were taught as children. With Ernest Renan it was not to be thus. Long before he had taken up Hebrew or could tell what the critics beyond Rhine were making of the Bible, he had quitted his hereditary moorings and was drifting out to sea.

From his letters this important conclusion, which seems to be denied in his *Reminiscences,* may be safely drawn. To his mother, of course, he gives no hint of the doubts that assail him. But they find expression in carefully chosen language when he is talking on paper with Henriette. In a year, he tells her (Sept. 15, 1842), he had learned as much as the human race learns in a century. The result is chiefly negative, indeed; but philosophy, as the Germans handle it, compels men to see the great problems if it does not answer them; it teaches us to reason inflexibly and to look at all things without veils. He is enamored of Kant. If Henriette goes to Königsberg, let her make a pilgrimage to the old philosopher's tomb. Such was the outcome of Renan's first year at Issy.

While he was losing his way in this dark forest of speculation, poverty kept close at his heels. He had no money to buy German grammars; he could win acquaintance with Goethe and Schiller only by using a fellow-student's volumes. His clerical attire gave him much concern; not because it was a mark of the calling which he had begun to think unsuited to his talents and temperament, but because the single cassock, worn every day, showed too many patches. If he did not know where to find the fifteen or twenty francs required for his Teutonic dictionary and its auxiliary tomes, how could he secure the sixty-five which a decent soutane cost in those days?

A correspondence, touching and anxious, passed between him and the good mother away in Brittany, on this matter of Ernest's wardrobe. Henriette, in her grand but forlorn castle, among the far-off Polish woods, sent what means were at command; but we read with sympathy and sadness of Madame Veuve Renan putting together all the silver she had and dispatching it to Issy in April, 1843. It arrived at a critical moment. His superiors had invited Renan to receive the tonsure, which would have given him the rights and status of a cleric, though binding him to no farther step. Was it possible for him with a good conscience to accept? The question had a twofold bearing. His mother would suppose that, if he asked for delay, some natural feelings were at work within him. But, however that might be, the trouble was of another sort, and he knew it. His faith in Revelation had undergone a great shock.

Nothing is more characteristic in this lad of twenty than his discreet way of handling the persons with whom he came in contact. Smilingly, the later Renan ascribes it to his Jesuit politeness and clerical reserve. But there was another explanation. As a child he had witnessed how frail is the security of the very poor; he was alarmed when he thought of the wild waters raging outside that peaceful haven in which he lay sheltered; and he dreaded to make shipwreck of his existence. He was never insincere; but he acted with a peasant's wariness, finely touched by genius, moulding itself in every phrase and at each conjuncture on the qualities of those who could help or injure him. Not even with Henriette was he completely frank at the present stage. To his mother he speaks as if her advice would be almost decisive. She, poor woman, replies, " Ernest, my dear Ernest, obey the inspirations of grace." She would never be a hindrance to him. Her letters are beautiful in their warmth and simplicity. M. Gosselin decides that he ought to take the step. On May 12, 1843, he consents; but a warning word falls from his pen: he is " ready for the sacrifice "—we think of Racine's *Iphigénie*—however, he ends by assuring Mme. Renan that calm has returned after the storm.

In three weeks all is changed. His letter of consent, he writes home on June 6, was a " fatal " one; at the last moment he has drawn back. The page that follows is certainly the most moving and sincere that he ever achieved. It is one long cry of agony lest his mother should doubt the affection he bore her, and refuse to bless him, to pardon him; yet how, he reiterates passionately, could he be unfaithful to the voice of conscience? He meant every word of all this; but only an acknowledgment which would have terrified the unhappy woman, as if it were sacrilege, could henceforth clear up the situation. And he felt incapable of making it. Between these two hearts a dreadful ambiguity had fallen like a veil. M. Gosselin added a few lines, approving of Ernest's hesitation. The widow answered with infinite tenderness. She was resigned but not enlightened. And so the first crisis came to an end.

Excellent M. Gosselin, learned in ancient lore, but not in the secrets of the modern spirit! His penitent might endeavor to lay bare his heart; it was a sealed book to the director. M. Gottofrey, a young priest of twenty-eight, with clear English features—he was not altogether French—sensitive and acute, perceived in this eternal reading and sharp argumentation of Renan symptoms which had escaped all others. In a scholastic tournament the young sceptic had broken a lance too vigorously against received views. His master ended the tilting-match at once, took him aside, and after enlarging on the perils of overmuch study, the futility of mere science, and the arrogance of Rationalism, cried in a passionate voice, "You are no Christian!" Renan was thunderstruck. He lay awake all night, and the terrible words echoed around him; they had gone right home. M. Gosselin did his best to comfort the troubled youth. M. Manier, sensible and moderate, advised him not to get lost in details; the Christian religion should be judged as a whole. This amiable man seems to have felt that Ernest had no vocation to the priesthood; for he was the first to hint that in the Ecole Normale his gifts as a teacher might be employed to edification.

This episode we have related at some length as offering a genuine clue to events which were afterward thrown out of perspective by Renan's Oriental studies. His faith was eclipsed, and in fact all but extinguished, by the new view in philosophy which he was deriving partly from Malebranche and yet more from what he could ascertain of German metaphysics. Though he made his own Descartes' abstract and inflexible rule of evidence—clear ideas—the sovereign conception to which he was yielding is rather a tendency than a formula. Science, he felt, was the only certain truth; everything else an hypothesis or a dream. By pure physical induction, founded on experience, the world might be interpreted and subdued, or else not at all.

Such is the language of Bacon; and Malebranche added that in the order of facts no special interpositions of the Divine Will are to be allowed. In other words, general laws must be identified with God's Providence. This recondite axiom, to which Malebranche gave an orthodox meaning, appears again and again in Renan's treatises; we may term it his great first truth, never proved but assumed as undeniable. Followed out to its consequences, it seemed to make the name and idea of Deity superfluous. The order of facts is sufficient for itself; what more do we want? Miracle and revelation cannot be admitted, since they would break the supreme, all-encompassing law, and disclose personality other than our own in the universe. Thus Renan argued, substituting an ideal system for the living God. From this ground he never retreated and never advanced. Only a year or two went by before he came to realize, and joyfully to maintain, the principle of scientific Atheism, which he was now unconsciously making his own. We ought, nevertheless, to bear in mind that philosophers of schools so different as were Leibnitz and Stuart Mill, would not have allowed his reasoning. To quote only the latter: "Science," observes Mill, "contains nothing repugnant to the supposition that every event which takes place results from a specific volition of the presiding Power, provided that this Power adheres in its particular volitions to general laws laid down by itself."

But there was nothing more distasteful to this fluctuating elusive temper than statements he could not recall. Though science had become his only source of truth, he manipulated its assumptions with a poet's freedom; when least original in matter, he was always himself in manner. We can never mistake a page written by him, even at this youthful stage, for any other man's; it is always classical in expression, tinged with subdued light as in a dream, self-controlled, and, even where it seems agitated, imperturbable. Renan was kind-hearted but not passionate; he could scarcely endure the soldier's trade, which courted, as well as inflicted, wounds and slaughter. He sought no authority, felt no enthusiasm for any propaganda, did all he knew to make his vision achromatic; then he sat down by the side of the process, watching how it would turn out.

Life thus became an experiment in chemistry, the will counting as a cipher, to be eliminated before anything was done. But while his conceit of himself as a purely reasoning machine proved fatal to Renan's Christianity, his imagination took fire at the mystic spring of German romance. For it would be the easiest matter in the world to show that Kant, but much more Fichte and Hegel, had but thrown into severe logical forms the old Pantheism, or mystery of the All and One, which colors every Teutonic writer of name, from Eckhardt and Behmen to Angelus Silesius.   Strictly-measuring science did not invent it, and cannot be charged with it.   The Faust legend, which even now captivated Renan, is poetry, not experiment, a flower of the fancy which never blossomed out of modern testing-tubes.   That which tempts the physical explorer to disbelieve in God, is his own absorption in disclosures where personality does not count. Whether we may deal after this method with religion is, to say the least, a problem; all men except an inconsiderable few have until now decided against it, or have taken their whole nature, moral and mental, as a guide to the divine.

And our young scholar did that, too.   The flash of lightning, he says, came and went again, leaving him unaffected.   He decided on entering St. Sulpice.   Henriette had forwarded by his brother Alain five hundred and fifty francs to defray his holiday at home and the cost of new clothes.   He spent a happy two months in Brittany, and, on October 13, 1843, took up his abode in the gaunt barrack-like building which occupies the site of M. Olier's seminary.   Within, all things were as that self-denying founder had left them.   M. Garnier, the superior-general, was upward of eighty-four. He had known M. Emery, Napoleon's favorite; he spoke of " Monsieur Bossuet " and " Monsieur Fénelon," as if the last of the Doctors had been calling on him yesterday. M. Hugon had served as acolyte when Talleyrand was consecrated in 1788, and the Saturday after had accused himself in confession of " rash judgment concerning the piety of a holy bishop." For M. d'Autun had behaved, during the ceremony, with scant reverence.

These excellent men offered a contrast to the raptures and singularities of M. Pinault and the other " saints " at Issy. They were neither mystics nor metaphysicians. M. Garnier, an Oriental scholar of enormous learning, had written *cahiers,* or lectures, sound on points of language, but untouched by modern criticism. He did not teach now; his pupil and successor was a tiny Breton, M. Le Hir. This orthodox luminary, who died in 1868 on the eve of the Vatican Council, to which he had been invited, knew the latest opinions at Tübingen, had examined the *Leben Jesu* of David Frederick Strauss, and, according to Renan, was perfectly candid in his quotations, while remaining as orthodox as ever. A saint and a *savant,* M. Le Hir could appropriate from Gesenius or Ewald whatever he deemed to be not incompatible with his creed. But in questions of divinity other masters ruled over him, German Catholics illustrious at that time, such as Möhler and the rising school of Munich. He had passed beyond the "old French Scholasticism," we are told—a system which Renan took for the one and only standard of belief, with consequences disastrous to him as to it.

This Gallican school, it must be remarked, has played in modern Catholic movements a part not unlike that of Calvinism elsewhere; by its excessive and forbidding formulas it has called out a reaction not less exaggerated, tending on the one side to infidelity, on the other to superstition. Its fatal defect was the severance between dogma and history. It knew nothing of development. It reduced Church and Bible to a code in which at the close of propositions, often debatable, still oftener not sealed with supreme authority, and detached from the living context in which alone their importance could be estimated, the formula "Est de fide" (it is matter of faith) appeared with a frequency as great as that of the death-penalty in secular enactments. French divines were narrow, forensic, curiously ignorant of the laws upon which ecclesiastical growth had gone forward. Time and change they did not allow among their categories; and they assumed that all men, everywhere, moved on the same level of understanding. When Ernest Renan brought his new idea of science face to face with their old theology, a conflict was inevitable and speedily broke out.

At St. Sulpice the rule of freedom prevailed to a degree which contrasted singularly with Napoleon's iron-bound institutions; it was a house founded rather on the old independent University of the Middle Ages than on the military code which reigns supreme over all State-schools in France. A young man, left to his own devices, might pass years without receiving direction from his superiors; the machine went on of itself, and there seems to have existed no *espionage* in the establishment at Paris. On the other hand, a certain coldness dwelt in the atmosphere; friendships did not easily spring up among strangers brought together as in an hostelry from the four corners of the land. Renan was more lonely than ever. During his two years of residence he lived as a hermit in the great city. Acquaintance he had scarcely any at all. Once a week he trudged along the Rue Vaugirard with his companions to spend an afternoon at Issy, according to the good old monastic rule which is observed by colleges abroad, of giving the scholars a day's *villegiatura* by way of relief from the city air. He did little else than read, reflect, write home, and fix his

mental attitude on the problems of Christian history which were now troubling him.   From the
abstract discussions of first principles he had advanced into a thicket where innumerable questions
of fact solicited his attention.   Yet he yielded so
far as to accept the tonsure at Christmas, 1843,
from Mgr. Affre, Archbishop of Paris, who was
martyred on the barricades five years later.   His
director had taken the responsibility of a step
which appeared only becoming if Renan was to
continue his studies at the Church's expense.
Minor orders followed on June 5, 1844.   Madame Renan felt supremely happy.   But her son
was approaching a decisive term—the subdia-
conate—which would have bound him as by
vow to a single life and permitted no turning
back again.   To faith all things are possible;
how if he had already made shipwreck of his
faith?

What is peculiar in this young man's falling
away from a creed so venerable and majestic, is
the silence, the utter solitude, in which he undid
every link of the golden chain.   Others as gifted
as he went over to modern ideas, but on crowded
paths and with loud acclaim.   Victor Hugo,
George Sand, Lamennais, drew all eyes upon their
defection.   Alfred de Musset, the " son of his
century," told the secret of many a French lad

when he wrote: " In my young days, innocent as I was and simple, vice came before me as a world admirable and immense. The moment I could, I plunged into it with delight." In lycées beyond counting, the tone had been to disbelieve in God, hate Christ, and practise the forbidden. But while from such a discipline Lacordaire came out to be champion of a despised religion, this other lonely youth, modest, edifying, submissive to rule, could not find in his Christian bringing up any motives that would countervail the objections of unbelievers.

He disliked Voltaire, then and always. He felt a strong repugnance to the campaign which Michelet and Edgar Quinet, renowned University professors, were directing in those years against the Catholic Church. But he felt an invincible prejudice which would not suffer him to admit Revelation as a fact, or miracles as probable; and thus in details he was at one with Voltaire and the *Encyclopædia*. Antecedent presumptions, trust in a good God, which the devout have relied upon, and to which Newman ascribed a weight only to be put aside by self-contradiction in the message or impossibility in its announcements, were made by Renan, somewhat after the fashion of Hume, reasons for doubting. He demanded proof such as might satisfy a board of physi-

cians and which amounted to ocular demonstration. When that was not forthcoming, he renounced the Gospel.

These thoughts, which float up slowly to the
surface of his correspondence, filled his mind between October, 1844, when he returned from vacation, and the conclusive moment a year later that
saw him leaving St. Sulpice. " Terrible doubts "
had, indeed, assailed him as he went up to the
altar and was repeating the words of the Psalm,
" The Lord is the portion of mine inheritance,"
while the Archbishop clipped his hair in token of
that dedication. He put them from him, but they
were not silenced. Reason, he learned in St.
Thomas Aquinas, had its claims; it must prove
the credibility of Revelation and discover grounds
for submitting to the Church. But he found in
the mediæval system a strange likeness to its vast
cathedrals. Therein he beheld " grandeur, wide
and empty spaces, but nothing solid." What were
its arguments? He answered, " triumphant syllogisms built on the void." What was its fatal defect? Surely the " want of historical criticism due
to the confounding of dates and environment."
He was mastering Hebrew and applying his new-
found knowledge to the Bible-narratives, not in
the least as an original student, but with ready
acquiescence in the methods of his German text-

books.   Under that light the supernatural faded
away; every form of Christian dogma perished;
of religion itself nothing was left save some scattered moral elements, without transcendent source,
or divine sanction, or scope beyond this world.
The critic stood aloft on a heap of ruins.   In the
endeavor to find out why he believed, he had
ceased to believe in anything.

Now, then, Renan looked about for an issue
which would take him without observation from
one camp to another.   He had got leave to attend
the lectures of M. de Quatremère, at the Collège
de France, to his mother's alarm but his own gratification.   A sign of the coming tempest falls on
his page; he has no desire to begin reciting his
Breviary, and therefore will not be a subdeacon
yet.   We turn to the correspondence with his sister, and find him a little more open.   He had
called the tonsure an " immolation," which must
have awakened in Henriette the feeling that Ernest had confidences to make, if she would but
encourage him.   Two years previously, in March,
1843, she had written, " I blame myself not
seldom for searching into your most intimate
thoughts, and leading you to search; but how can
I conceal what is in my heart?"   The last months
at Issy, she is now told, in a letter dated April 16,
1844, were vexed by unkindness from his com-

panions. He dislikes the clerical profession; he
is not of a temper to live with common and in-
triguing spirits. M. Dupanloup has offered him
a post in St. Nicolas; but " everyone knows what
a masterful man Dupanloup is." He could, indeed, join the Sulpicians, and they would welcome
so successful a scholar; but he prefers a solitary
and private life, independence if possible, and the
means of research to be obtained in Paris alone.
What does Henriette advise?

Among these considerations one which took
from them all significance had found expression.
" I have never hesitated," says the young man,
" except as desiring to know *where* the truth was,
or whether it commanded that I should serve it in
the Church, notwithstanding the human difficulties
which I could not hide from myself. But, whether
I embraced the clerical state or not—I will say
more—let my sentiments be what they might concerning the religion in which I believed that I had
found the truth—a life serious and retired, far
from superfluities and pleasures, would have determined my choice; and that is what I promised "
—on taking the tonsure. He adds prophetically,
" Should I ever become a vain and futile creature,
attached to the despicable rewards of a day, or to
an opinion more wretched still (I do not speak
of glory, which is no vanity if we can wait for it),

then I should hold that I had been faithless to my engagement."

Henriette had thrown out a hope of some travelling tutorship in Germany. It would give him a respite, should nothing better fall in his way. But she was emphatically against his entering St. Nicolas or joining St. Sulpice. And he must have time. With a generosity that her brother could never forget, she promised him a year—two years, if need be—of freedom at her own cost; he should see a little of the world; and if he gave up the priesthood, there was no dishonor in obeying a sensitive conscience. Her letter of February 28, 1845, in which these plans are debated, is a model of passionate but restrained eloquence, not stirring the deep chord of doubt by so much as a finger-tip, but insisting that he cannot act until he has arrived at a " clear and individual decision." Unlike Ernest, she knew her own mind, while he could perceive reasons on both sides and was " cruelly perplexed."

His answer, on April 11, 1845, is, at last, candid. " If the end of man were joy," he says finely, " life would be intolerable to those who are denied it; but when we have fixed our term in a higher world we are less troubled by what passes below." Then a note is sounded which was to echo by and by in his most famous volume, " I

have comforted myself as one that suffers for conscience' sake and for virtue. The thought of that
Jesus in the Gospel, so pure, fair, and calm, so
little understood by those who worship Him, has
been above all a wonderful support to me." We
are put in mind of George Eliot translating with
tears, before the crucifix, from the *Leben Jesu,*
which was to make such consoling thoughts impossible for a great and unhappy multitude. Renan goes on, " I don't think that I ever told you
the real motives . . . I will tell you now.
Take it in a single word: I do not believe enough."
The Catholic Church was once to him the absolute
truth. Could it be so still, he would devote himself to it. But reason is awake; it puts in its
claim, and the absolute has vanished. Catholicism holds him no more.

" I shall love it, I shall admire it always," he
exclaims; " it has cherished and given joy to my
childhood; it has made me what I am; its morality (I mean that of the Gospel) shall ever be my
rule; I shall ever have in aversion the sophists
that assail it with slander and bad faith; they comprehend it even less than others who receive it
with closed eyes. Jesus, above all, shall be my
God. But when we come down from this pure
Christianity . . . forgive me, Henriette—I
do not cling to these thoughts, but I doubt; and

it does not depend on me to see otherwise than I do see. . . . That is the only cause which keeps me from being a priest."

Not celibacy, then, but the *sagrifizio d'intelletto,* as Cognat truly remarks, was the spectre before whose presence Renan drew back terrified. We must even go beyond this, and assert in him a dislike of all affirmations not compelled by evidence as of the sun at noonday. The priesthood was a life-long affirmation; he desired, at most, only such engagements as might be laid aside when he suspected their hollowness; and an instructive parallel opens between this manner of binding oneself to truth and the so-called Free Love which in George Sand's best-known period struck the keynote of her novels.

But the same thing meets us everywhere in modern life and literature. The Zeitgeist, a prisoner of time, shudders at " the constant service of the antique world," whether it was loyal to God or man. That a rustic without experience, dazzled by abstract reasoning on all sides of him, should not have seen the emptiness of such time-serving, may be pardonable. His masters, devout but little versed in that science which F. von Schlegel has well termed the philosophy of life, could neither comprehend nor answer him. Their apologetics were exhausted. As for the splendid and vital fact of historic religion, from which the divine personality of Jesus could be torn only to deny Him in the end, as Unitarians must do, Renan possessed no light in himself whereby to discern its value. He had acted and suffered too little; he had been dwelling not in the dark, but in shadowland, too long for even a genius like his to measure the reality of things. And Henriette, who had more to undergo, never fell into the mood of artistic trifling which at length absorbed all that was austere and fine in her brother's character.

This judgment is not simply mine. It has been uttered by men as unlike one another as Tholuck and M. Séailles, the latter of whom signalizes this period in Renan's life as heroic. To go on with our story. Henriette, we may surmise, had been waiting for this confession. She replied, June 1, 1845, "I understand; I sympathize." She had written to Vienna, and taken steps to get him a tutorship; but whatever came of them, she adds, "when certain ideas have been ventilated, they leave their trace. You are moving on a fresh path." Her counsel would be to give up St. Sulpice, continue the study of Eastern languages under M. de Quatremère, and fix himself in Paris. A young man could live on twelve hundred francs a year; she will find them for Ernest, whose future is her chief concern. But their mother? Henriette was for plain-dealing; not so this apprehensive and less daring spirit, who could not face the tragedy which seemed imminent. The formidable secret had been kept between them. He now talked of shaking off a burden, the clerical state, which destiny had laid upon him, and of sacrificing all to duty. Could he not, however, take his degree and prepare for the Ecole Normale? But he must surely wait till October; he must come back to St. Sulpice. He was then writing two days before the last vacation which he intended to pass as a cleric in Brittany.

His sister, addressing him by means of a friend, so as to escape Madame Renan's observation, did not wholly approve. Let him return to Paris in lay attire, take a lodging, and have done with the Seminary. Alain, who lived at St. Malo, would procure what was needful. When she wrote in an open letter, "Take your degree," such would be its real meaning.

The poor mother looked on all this while, with distress and growing perplexity. She felt that her boy did not lay bare his heart to her as of old. One day, as he was reading by her side, she snatched the book out of his hand with an exclamation, "Ah, Ernest, your ideas will make them fling you on the pavement!" It was her continual but

Ernest Renan's Birthplace at Tréguier.

hitherto unspoken dread. She recited instances; the lot of a discarded cleric was, indeed, too often miserable. But they talked of the journey over the Rhine, which never came to pass in the way she dreamed. Ernest felt that he could not throw off the cassock. He was in extreme agitation, and Henriette, thinking him irresolute, rebuked his want of courage in a letter dated October 10, 1845, on the eve of her departure for Italy with the Zamoyski. By that time all was over, and Renan had left the Catholic Church.

His resolution was not taken until the closing days of September. To his dear Breton masters he could not enter upon questions which *he* decided by weighing evidence in critical scales, and which *they* forestalled by the authority of tradition. As little would his mother have believed that he was giving up religion because, according to some German expositors, the Messianic interpretation of the Psalms was unfounded, or Gesenius appeared to him a better judge of what Isaiah meant than St. Thomas Aquinas had been. Why, it may be asked, did Renan seek no alternative in Liberal or Unitarian views? At home he gave up receiving the Sacraments. He meditated on the large horizons which Herder especially opened before his enchanted gaze. Might he not be, then, as Herder was, an enlightened modern while remaining a Christian minister? During these two months he felt like a Protestant. But logic triumphed. A secret voice whispered in his ear, "You are no longer a Catholic; your soutane is a falsehood; take it off."

On the other hand, he was no professor at Halle or Tübingen; to the French Huguenot Church he had never been drawn. And, after all, those who deny the supernatural cannot be Christians in any definite or historical sense. If the solitary dreamer was borne up by an ideal which he named Jesus, that cloud-phantom did not resemble the divine object of faith. Among Renan's former instructors at Tréguier only one caught a glimpse into his mind. "Ah," he said, "I always fancied they made you study too hard." His custom of reciting the Psalms in Hebrew astonished them; did he want to turn Jew? He despatched a long account of his ideas to the director in Paris who had failed, though with the best of intentions, to lead him out of the maze. "I did hope," said he, "that when I had gone round the circle of doubt, I should come back to the point from which I started; I have lost that expectation altogether; I could return to Catholicism only by abjuring my reason." He had often been tempted to revolt against so dangerous a guide. But how could he? The Catholic creed was a bar of iron; would there ever be set up among Frenchmen a rational, a critical Christianity? At all events, for him the priesthood was out of the question.

To all this his director had no reply that would avail. Catholic truth was one thing, Rationalism another. "Then indeed," Newman had written in 1839, "will be the stern encounter, when two real and living principles, simple, entire, and consistent, one in the Church, the other out of it, at length rush upon each other, contending not for names and words, or half views, but for elementary notions and distinctive moral characters." This was what had happened to Renan; but never had a Church been less prepared to meet such a crisis than the French in 1845. Its knowledge of the situation was deplorably inadequate. Of Biblical studies it had no grasp; philosophy had become to it a string of formulas; it saw only in the dimmest distance what other Churches and nations were doing with religion. To this effect wrote the late Mgr. d'Hulst, who would not willingly have darkened the melancholy picture. Certain it is that we cannot recall a name in those disastrous years among French divines which united learning with insight, or anyone who would set forth in modern and effective terms the ancient beliefs. Lacordaire, for example, is a memory of which

Catholics are proud. But Lacordaire knew no German; neither would his impassioned rhetoric make up for the want of exegesis, the limited acquaintance with history, primitive or Eastern, the defective psychology, all of which at that time bore hard upon ecclesiastical training. And who else was there?

Ernest bade his mother farewell; called in St. Malo for Henriette's last letters; and, still wearing his cassock, arrived at St. Sulpice on October 6, 1845. He found that the critical moment was at hand. Mgr. Affre contemplated setting up immediately a house of studies in which Renan should be one of the professors. The young man was told to call upon his Archbishop the same day and give him a reply. A few hours later the prelate came to St. Sulpice, and sent for him. Renan consulted his friends. By their advice he declined the interview. But his superiors knew that he did not mean to stay at the Seminary; and as evening fell, he went down the steps for the last time in his cassock, crossed the square rapidly, and made his way to the neighboring hotel, or lodging-house, of Mlle. Céleste. The change to lay attire was not at once completed. But in this abrupt fashion the unknown had been faced and Renan had flung himself upon the pavement of Paris.

Three days afterward, as we have set down

elsewhere, Newman submitted to the Catholic Church at Littlemore. His reason had convinced him that faith is indispensable; that Revelation is a fact; that of alternatives one must be chosen; and that Church, Bible, religion stand or fall together. He embraced a consistent scheme of life, which had survived long ages. Renan, taking the other path, went into the wilderness, whither we must now follow him.

CHAPTER III

THE SCHOLAR IN PARIS

BEFORE setting out on her own journey, Henriette had forwarded to Mlle. Ulliac in Paris a bill of fifteen hundred francs for Ernest's use, payable November 10 at Messrs. Rothschild's. He was not, therefore, destitute. He could always fall back on this little store, although he seems never to have taken from it. The Sulpicians, too, behaved with a kindness which almost overcame him, surprising as it was, he thought, in men so orthodox toward a fugitive from their house. They procured an honorable post for him in the Collège Stanislas, the head of which, M. Gratry, was eminent in literature and mathematics. Dupanloup advised him not to refuse it, adding, " My poor purse is at your service; I wish I could offer you something more valuable." The assistance was declined with no less good feeling than that which had prompted it. Renan, bent on sparing his mother, made trial of M. Gratry and the Collège Stanislas.

He found the rector fascinating but chimerical,

wholly unversed in his own branches of knowledge.
Their conversations were a perpetual misunderstanding on the part of Gratry. But this arrange-
ment could not last. Renan was expected to appear, like the other masters, in soutane. That
he would not do; on All Souls' Day he left the
college, and took up his abode in the Quartier
St. Jacques as a private tutor without salary. He
was lodged and boarded; he had his own room;
two hours a day with seven pupils paid for this
not disagreeable entertainment; and he would have
felt happy, but that Madame Renan was in great
trouble about him, while the strange, cold atmosphere chilled him after so long a seclusion. His
poor mother sang in her Breton solitude of her
Joseph whom wild beasts had devoured; his reticence had been a trial; but he could not yet bring
himself to be open with her. Their correspondence during the next months is painful reading.
At last, in March, 1846, Henriette, who detested
concealments, explained his conduct in a letter
which sums up the story.

By this time Ernest had taken his bachelor's
degree, not without some official embarrassment,
due to the place where he had been trained. For
St. Sulpice was not a Government school. M.
Jullien, the Chinese scholar, was of use to him;
others had remarked his quickness to learn. At

twenty-three seldom had a young provincial won so much notice. Henriette, after dwelling on all this, foretells that he will be distinguished and superior in whatever calling he follows. She was writing from Rome. In 1846 the Polish peasantry broke out against the nobles, who had treated them from of old like serfs. Count Zamoyski, as it appears, was forewarned, and thought well to start on a long holiday in Southern Europe. Some of the nobles were murdered shortly after at Zamosk. And there was hope that Henriette might return to her people in France—a hope deferred, however, until September, 1850, when Ernest met her in Berlin and took her home to Paris.

Ten years of exile had given her the looks of middle age, though she was but eight and thirty. " Of the charm," says her brother, " which had been hers when bidding me farewell in the parlor of St. Nicolas, nothing remained but a delightful expression, the token of unspeakable kindness." She had lived long enough in Rome to feel its attraction. Her creed was a pure Theism; and though she did not permanently influence her brother's opinions, while she lived the serious note which we miss from his later writings was, on the whole, dominant.

To the correspondence with Henriette succeeds,

before long, an almost equally interesting exchange of thought between Ernest and a new friend, Marcellin Berthelot. From November, 1845, they were next-door neighbors in the " obscure lodging-house " of the Rue des Deux Églises, where Renan passed three years and a half, teaching without salary. In power and accomplishments the young men were, perhaps, on a level; in temper they differed widely. After so fierce a struggle with his Elohim—to speak Hebraically —the recalcitrant Levite could still remind his former associate Cognat, that " We are happy in defiance of logic." M. Carbon had perceived that the silent and seemingly morose Breton was by nature of a gay disposition, though he could be resigned to the inevitable. He was resolute and sanguine; but little given to " particular friendships," as the monastic phrase went, chiefly because he found occupation in his own thoughts, which he deemed equal to other men's actions; nor would he swerve, when he had once made up his mind, to please anybody.

Berthelot, four years his junior (born in 1827), is a more attaching figure. His mother was of Paris; his father, the son of a peasant on the banks of the Loire, had taken a degree in medicine and practised in a poverty-stricken neighborhood, close to St. Jacques la Boucherie. Too tender-hearted for ambition, the doctor was always poor, and, says Marcellin, " from the age of ten years I have been troubled by the uncertainty of the future." In his friendships, according to Henriette, who knew and valued him, there appeared all the sensitive delicacy of a woman. The father, Gallican in his religious principles, astonished Renan by his republican sentiments, which were a new experience for the Breton, himself willing to live under any Government, if it would only last. Marcellin, who shared these advanced views, cared nothing about antiquity, laid out a path for himself in science, and, thanks to his father's generous help, lived in a world of disinterested research until he was thirty. As a mere lad he counted among the most brilliant pupils of the Collège Henri IV; and in 1846 he won the highest prize in philosophy, though scarcely nineteen.

Already a Freethinker, he was drawn toward Renan by a certain likeness in their fortunes, by his " mild and serious expression," and by the energy which he threw into his daily work, often prolonged into the small hours of the morning. They were both determined not to mortgage their freedom, as too many have done in France, by entering on the career of administration. Young, ignorant of life, eager to know whatever could be known, they met only to discuss the great problems. Berthelot initiated his friend into the secrets of chemistry, and enlarged on the prospect of a new social order. Renan persuaded Marcellin to buy a Hebrew Testament, the leaves of which he did not cut, and expounded theology to him from the critic's point of sight. "A few months were enough," says the unfrocked cleric, "to relegate the vestiges of the faith among our memories." Very soon they could not have told which were their several parts in the ideas that came to them.

But Renan had begun to write. Victor Cousin, whose great fame was over, but whose intellectual curiosity never slackened, and Victor Le Clerc, the historian, encouraged him to make good use of his Eastern lore. Under such auspices, he gained an entrance to the world of letters and libraries. In 1847 he completed his degrees at the University. That same year he presented to the Academy of Inscriptions his *General History of the Semitic Languages*. It is a bold and speculative work, original in method, and it won the Volney prize. We feel in reading it that the author will never consent to be a mere *savant;* he throws out conjectures, lays open the soul of Arab and Aryan, and explains religion by race, landscape, and psychology.

On February 24, 1848, the street riots broke

out before which Louis Philippe ran to England,
leaving the Tuileries in the hands of a mob.
Whoever wishes to see that shameful page of history as it was enacted, let him study *A Sentimental
Education*, by Gustave Flaubert.   Renan, at that
time, was attending the lessons on Sanscrit of Burnouf, at the Collège de France.   On the 25th he
found the lecture-hall transformed to a guard-
room.   For one moment he, too, was tempted by
the fever of the barricades.   But he said to himself, "Science is a religion; it never loses its value,"
and making his way along the armed streets, he
went to Burnouf's private residence, where the
Sanscrit lesson was resumed.   Then came the
"Days of June," during which the working-men
of Paris fought the middle class and were defeated with frightful slaughter.   To his friend
Berthelot Renan writes on the 26th that it was
worse than the St. Bartholomew; that he would
himself have been prepared to join the National
Guard in putting down anarchy, but the Guard
had become an executioner; and that, guilty as
were "these poor maniacs," more guilty still were
the men who had made of them helots and brutes.

A few days later he visited the battle-field—St.
Antoine, the Rue St. Jacques, which goes from
the Pantheon to the Quais, the Place of the Bastille.   His account, uncommonly picturesque for

Renan, is worth quoting. " The barricades," he says, " were like regular fortresses, with salient angles, one succeeding another at every fifty yards. The square of the Bastille offered a dreadful scene of chaos. All the trees were cut down or shattered by bullets; houses pulled to the ground or still in flames; actual towers built up with scaffold poles, vehicles overturned, paving-stones piled in heaps. In the midst of all that, the people stupefied, hardly knowing what they were about in such unimaginable circumstances; soldiers asleep on the flags, almost under the feet of passers-by; the rage of the conquered showing itself under apparently quiet looks; the disorder of the conquerors as they cleared their way across the barricades overthrown; and elsewhere the compassion of the public who were asking charity for the wounded and linen to dress their wounds . . . it was a sight of sublime originality, naked man face to face with his fellow, nothing left but his primitive instincts."

But the spectacle gave him a shock. He had seen it too close at hand. He could not love these new Barbarians. How shall they cease to be proletarians, nay, bourgeoisie? In what way can the " people " be civilized, lest they destroy all things of price like Franks or Vandals? These questions haunted Renan during the seven months from

November, 1848, until June of the year following, which he spent on a large and somewhat ungainly volume, *The Future of Science*. It unfolds
a Utopian programme; but all he ever knew or
dreamed may be traced across its pages, rudely
sketched, exuberant, or inchoate, wanting the touch
of his mature style, for he was not yet an artist.
He felt convinced that scientific research, not abstract speculation, would discover how mankind
had originated. But if so, it must not pause until
it dealt with history, philology, myth, and legend,
the primitive, spontaneous man who had created
our governing ideas. This brings him to the
Christian origins, on which " the most important
book of the nineteenth century " is waiting to be
written. Nay, he will write it himself, unless
death or some other fatality interposes.

This pregnant volume remained in manuscript
until 1890. Renan's best friends did not advise
publication; and further experience led him to ac-
quiesce in their counsel. The Republic had no
need of critics. But, on the motion of M. Le
Clerc, he was sent by the Academy of Inscriptions
to Italy in November, 1849.

The French had driven Garibaldi out of Rome;
and their soldiers were holding the city, while
Pius IX was still at Gaeta. This expedition, of
which Renan became a member, had for its object

antiquarian research. He accepted the mission with joy. " It will be an epoch in my life," he wrote to Berthelot, " as an artist and a man." Such, indeed, it turned out to be. On November 9 he arrived in the Eternal City. He came back by Turin at the close of May, 1850. Six months of a pilgrimage in search of the beautiful formed a second or third stage of his intellectual training, which his correspondence, in those years not scanty, describes with ever-growing enthusiasm.

Rome enchanted him. His prejudices melted away before the marvellous apparition; he was conquered by the Madonna, whose picture he saw at every street-corner, adorned with lights and flowers. His very religion rose from the dead, a shadowy but subduing phantom. He had never grasped what a popular faith really is in a nation that knows no other. Faith and civilization— not in the base mechanical sense—attained in Rome to " an incomparable poetry, height, ideal-ism." In the French temperament to cultivate ideals was to invent formulas; here it meant the plastic arts, and life itself was religion. The at-mosphere had something antique; comfort did not exist, but who minded its absence? Paris was pro-fane, Rome everlastingly sacred. The Revolution, as understood in France, would never take root south of the Alps. It was a Jacobin idea that

the Catholic Church must be annihilated; but for
Italians to be orthodox was everything; they would
defend their superstitions to the death. As for
the French army of occupation, Voltairian or
democratic, the people detested its ways, and only
the middle class, a small minority, was in league
with it.

These observations teach us that Renan had
good eyes under his heavy eyelids. We may compare some other of his pages, denouncing the clerical government, with Lamennais' *Affaires de
Rome,* in the spirit of which they are cast. But
that which he gained for his own benefit was a
revelation of the old classic existence, untroubled
by industry, spending its hours in the Forum,
everywhere surrounded by creations of an art
which ministered far more to public life than to
private luxury. From these days we may reckon
his attachment to the world of which printed
classics had but shown him the least remarkable
aspect. More and more his vision turned toward
the past, beyond what he afterward called the
" frightful adventure of the Middle Ages," to a
seemingly nobler antiquity. When he went down
to Naples, the landscape gave him a setting for
his future treatment of the Apocalypse; but he was
disgusted with so gross a population and its vil-
lainous taste. The ruins of Pæstum, famed for

its temples and its roses in the time of Virgil, filled him with melancholy. One civilization had perished thus; what would be the fate of our own?

He wrote again from Monte Cassino, in January, 1850. The Benedictines were Italian patriots, who vied in enthusiasm with Gioberti, Rosmini, Ventura—priests and leaders at that time celebrated. But Padre Tosti, not long since the counsellor of Pius IX, was in a sort of exile at Rome; the monks trembled for their abbey; meanwhile they discussed German thought and French revolutions. In one of their cells Renan found the *Leben Jesu* of Strauss. He admired their zeal; he smiled at their Guelfic dreams. The salvation of Italy, he declares, will come from its monks; but they must not think of imitating his own countrymen. He saw Tosti later, but did not forebode the long martyrdom of that brave spirit, which ended only with his life not many years ago.

Returning to Rome after a hasty survey of Florence, and a day never to be forgotten at lovely Pisa, the French traveller, who had been received in audience with his companions by Pius IX, awaited the Pontiff's entrance with curiosity. He conjectured that his welcome would be a cold one, and merely official. But, on April 12, 1850, he was present in the square of St. John Lateran when Pius arrived from the South; and he beheld a scene of frantic rejoicing all round him, with cries as violent as they were momently sincere. We may be permitted to add a sequel. Twenty years later, on September 19, 1870, the present writer happened to witness from the Scala Santa Pius IX driving into the same square for the last time. He had come to ascend the sacred steps and to bless his little army, a detachment of which was holding the Gate of St. John against the Italian troops. But now there was no wild shouting, and the Pope in red mantle looked deadly pale as he raised his hand in benediction. Next morning Rome was taken; Pius IX became a prisoner in the Vatican, which he never afterward quitted. Renan observes that the population, whose transports were so indescribable on a day of triumph, would have insulted their sovereign had he been mounting the scaffold. In good and bad the Romans were extreme.

He travelled into Umbria, where he praised Assisi beyond all for its beauty and pathos, calling St. Francis " the Christ of the Middle Age." Toward the end of May, 1850, he arrived in Venice. Venice, he remarks with profound truth, is the lagoon, not the *terra ferma*. He admired it as a lovely flower which could not live in the modern air; but, again, he thought it more Byzantine than classic, and the time came when he stigmatized the Place of St. Mark as something barbarous. The Venetian people, by origin Gauls, were mixed with Slavs and Hungarians; he could not admire them as he did the " Athenians of Florence." However, in this part of his journey Renan discovered materials at Padua for the book which he was meditating on the great Spanish philosopher, Averroes, from whom that university derived much of its debased doctrine. At Milan the Emperor Napoleon and the Kingdom of Italy reigned still. A glance at Turin sufficed; and we find him once more in Paris, to which, as he told his mother in 1845, he clung for dear life.

In September, as already noted, he met his sister at Berlin, and brought her to the small apartment, in a garden overlooking the Carmelites, near the Val de Grace, where they lived six years. Henriette kept house for him with a Frenchwoman's graceful economy; she shared his studies and copied his manuscripts for the press. But she did more. By her severe and penetrating criticism she compelled him to lay aside whatever was hard or excessive in his first manner, to check his fondness for the satirical, and to be content with a simple, unalloyed French, akin to that of Port Royal, which had become her own standard. By this description we are led to think of Pascal; but Ernest Renan, though he writes as pure a language, did not compass the brief sententious style of the *Pensées;* he was always a little too malicious even for the *Lettres Provinciales.* " I had never suffered," he says, " and I found in the discreet smile, provoked by man's weakness or vanity, a certain wisdom." He pretends that he gave up the ironical habit; let the reader of his last writings and speeches agree, if he can.

Together they went into questions of French art and architecture. They visited Rouen, Rheims, and the country between, where the pointed style had attained its perfection. Henriette was happy, but she thought Ernest should be so too, and she advised him to marry, not without secret misgivings. He was familiar with a Dutch artist of repute, Ary Scheffer, and from that intimacy, says Berthelot, had derived new lights which added to his literary powers. M. Scheffer's niece, Cornélie, was highly accomplished, in every way the wife that Renan would have chosen. But now his sister's jealous affection led to an agitating episode, and some bitter days intervened. Ernest told Mlle. Cornélie that he would not marry unless Henriette were satisfied. The same evening he let his sister know what he had done. It was enough. She ran next morning to M. Scheffer's, gave her full consent, and all turned out for the best. It was on her savings that the household

depended. Renan was married in St. Germain
des Près on September 11, 1856; and the two
ladies, though in different ways, lived happy ever
after.

Versatile and indefatigable, the man himself,
who loved knowledge for its own sake, was yet
a minor in business. " I will write books," he
had said as a child. But he did not fancy that
they would secure him a livelihood. What was
his astonishment when, one day, M. Michel Lévy
came upstairs to his garret, praised certain of his
articles in the *Revue des Deux Mondes* and elsewhere, and offered terms for a collected issue!
He tells the story with a point of humor; gladly
the bargain was made, and thirty volumes followed in succession down to 1887. Eleven others,
marked posthumous, complete the record. Besides this great library, which commands a general
interest, we should take into account Renan's lectures in Hebrew, his share in the Academy of Inscriptions, and the volumes which he brought out
jointly with Victor Le Clerc on France in the
fourteenth century.

A robust constitution served him well. His appearance, we are told, was wanting in distinction.
He made no effort to shine at social gatherings,
though he could talk supremely well among the
elect. He cared little for money and shunned

advertisement. Scarcely did he affect to be a man
of letters. The circumstances which were to transform a secluded Oriental student into the most
popular anti-Christian of his time lay yet in the
future. Tempted by every branch of learning,
from Sanscrit, which he took up with Burnouf,
to Chinese and the Greek of the Middle Age, he
ran a risk—it may be said that he did not escape
it—which all *dilettanti* must encounter, of losing
himself among by-paths. *Averroes*, which was
published in 1852, proved almost a dull book;
but it was meant for those who read to be in-
structed, not to be passively entertained. By it
he won his degree as Doctor of Letters. The
History of the Semitic Languages opened a fruitful contrast between the genius of Israel or Ish-
mael and the Aryan capacity for abstract reasoning. It was the scholar's prelude to undertakings
more literary on the same great subject. First
in the collected *Studies of Religious History* of
1857, he approached the work which was to make
him famous, and startled the orthodox into a
suspicion that some new enemy, a Celsus or even
a Voltaire, was entering the field.

On the history of Israel, on the *Critical Historians of Jesus,* on the *Imitation* and the Bol-
landist *Lives of the Saints* he expressed his views
with a freedom which gave no small offence.

Toward F. D. Strauss he took up an attitude which seemed equivocal; but in declining to be a mythologist Renan made light of the Gospel facts. A charming fable had no need of testimony. Did we care whether the *Iliad* was founded on a veracious chronicle? The picture of a sublime character gains nothing, he said, by its resemblance to an actual hero.

Jean Jacques had thought otherwise. "My friend, it is not so that we invent," he tells us in the well-known passage, "it would be more inconceivable that a number of men had combined to fashion the Gospel than that one man had furnished its subject." Renan professed, in his correspondence at the seminary, to be relying altogether on historical motives. He had even written to Berthelot from Venice, "History is to me what reason is to you." But facts were now to him of no consequence, provided we could save the ideal in our imagination. Whether events have justified him, many of his desponding pages at an after period will show. His judgment of Feuerbach is curiously applicable to himself. "When he resolves to be an atheist, he is one devoutly and with a kind of unction." That sentence, which reminds us of Montaigne, might be printed as a running epigraph on every one of the forty volumes which amused, or fascinated, or shocked the innumerable readers of a romantic who protested against Romanticism, an idealist who strove in vain to be commonplace, an archangel ruined who could not forget the Heaven whence he had cast himself down.

To adverse comments he made no direct answer, but a subsequent volume, *Essays in Morals and Criticism,* which appeared in 1859, began with a preface which was marked by all his inimitable qualities and held out a challenge to dogmatic Christians not likely to be forgotten. He was sorry to give them scandal, but he believed in duty, which was not the art of being happy, and he quoted Kant. Then he enlarged upon the religion of the heart, disengaged from symbols, and expressed his delight in meeting with assailants whose faith appeared to be so lively. Religion might be permitted to indulge in some narrow ideas and an indifferent style; for himself he was a critic and he could pardon the Church when it said uncivil things of him. Renan proceeded to explain that in 1851 he had taken the French Revolution to be liberal in principle, but he could do so no longer. Its violence, its atomic conception of man and society, its lowering of culture, its destruction of initiative, had brought in the reign of mediocrity. There was need to reform 1789. He might be a pessimist; he acknowledged that his mood was not sanguine; for he could not believe that industry and the fine arts would flourish together, and the Great Exhibition gave him no comfort.

At last he took refuge in the poetry of the Celtic races—there was his ideal country, he cried in a lyric outburst. "O sires of the lowly tribe at whose hearth I learned to believe in the unseen —humble clan of peasants and mariners, to whom I owe it that I have kept the vigor of my spirit in a dead land, in an age without hope, ye doubtless have roamed over those enchanted seas where our father Brandan sought the Land of Promise. . . . Sometimes I regret that your bark, leaving Ireland or Cambria, did not run before other breezes. In my dreams I see those peaceful cities of Clonfert and Lismore, where I ought to have passed my days—poor Ireland!—borne up on the sound of thy bells, on the story of thy mysterious wanderings. . . . Let us find comfort in our fancies, our nobleness, our disdain. Who can tell whether our dreams may not be more true than reality? God is my witness, ye ancient sires, that my only joy is to imagine, as I sometimes do, that I am your very conscience, and that by me ye come to have a life and a voice!"

The eighty pages on Celtic bards and legends to which these words invite us, have never been surpassed in their faint elusive colors, their romance of history, their pleading tone. They found an echo with Matthew Arnold, whose eyes, we may conjecture, were opened by them to fresh and untrodden vistas; half a century ago they pointed to the Gaelic revival, with its poetry of resistance, its disdain for the vulgar modern spirit. As Augustin Thierry well observed, the prophetic fame of Cambria during the Middle Ages was won by the refusal of its bards to despair of their own future. The Celt may suffer defeat; he is never vanquished. Arthur will come again. " Almost every strong appeal to the supernatural," concludes Renan, " has been due to the nations that hope against hope." He cites the greatest, Israel. But his argument bears a deeper application, for it implies that religion is not of this world.

After the idealist comes the critic. Much as he owed to Victor Cousin, he made bold in the most flattering way imaginable to draw that celebrated man from a superior point of view. Cousin was the sparkling French professor, true descendant of Gorgias or Protagoras, bred up by the University in all the arts which could be displayed on a theatre. His world was Paris; and though he had once crossed the Rhine, luckily what he brought back of Hegel and Kant would never dam-

age his exquisite style. To old ideas he gave new
expression. Good French is so difficult that it
tempts one to say a great deal more than one
thinks. True, there is no need, if a man be skil-
ful, to offer it violence. But, then, a lecturer must
be eloquent and "theory in France springs up
armed"; among Germans it is otherwise. Philosophy does not look to consequences; but with a
crowd some diplomatic handling may be required.
M. Cousin had shown himself a real tactician of
the idea. His countrymen prefer form to substance; they judge reason by its political and social
tendencies; no wonder if in such a latitude systems
freeze into scholastic repetitions and the discovery
of unknown truth becomes impossible.

What is the cure for this? Renan, still praising
M. Cousin, would recommend an infusion of science, mathematics, and above all of history. Education is now only a training in literature, which
means declamation. But the history of the human
mind—not as an individual, which was the mistake of former studies—no, as it moves in nations
and epochs—that, says Renan, is the philosophy
we should acquire. Cousin defends the established
religion; what has he to tell us about dogma,
Bible, the contents of that for which he stands
up? Just nothing at all. In like manner he bows
to the French Revolution, which was but a Gallic

episode, not a European turning-point; and then, despairing of his own time, seek refreshment in the more heroic period of the Fronde. It is well. To pursue the ideal, though we should never attain to it, brings an abundant reward.

Those who would measure the resources of French phrase, should examine this piercing, yet perfectly well-mannered, essay side by side with M. Taine's on the same subject. In sentiment there is little difference; in delicacy and point Renan has all the advantage of a supple genius, disporting itself at ease. Taine is strong, satirical, somewhat forced; his blows are heavy as they are telling. But, at the age of thirty-five, the quondam Sulpician has polished his instrument like a born courtier; he knows its powers and uses it as an enchanted sword, irresistibly keen. In a moral aspect the sight is not pleasant, for Cousin had laid him under a debt of gratitude. His excuse might be that he was criticizing the University, drawing attention to the barrenness of purely French ideas. But why not choose another target?

In writing about Lamennais, his sympathy was more sincere; not that he admired Liberal Catholicism, which he reprobated in the name of St. Sulpice, " that suave and touching reminiscence of the past "; nor that he could away with democ-

Portion of a Letter Written by Renan in 1858.

racy, or trusted in any fanatical movement; but he understood his fellow-provincial. Lamennais thought he did well to be angry; his eloquent hatred was a burning sombre flame; he should have gone out from the Church by " the royal road of history and criticism," whereas he did but exchange an absolute creed for its opposite. One great thing he had wrought, *The Words of a Believer,* which men might praise without reserve on condition that they did not think of copying it. " I never read those stirring pages," said Renan, " without an impression of contagious magic "; their rude austerity, sudden tenderness, and languor in the midst of an overmastering rage, were absolutely Breton. Yet a " respectful irony " was something better. " Disdain," said the critic, " almost always produces a delicate style "; but anger is often in bad taste. Thus far the Epicurean who, yielding to a kindlier emotion, confesses that Lamennais' impatience was due to " the unrest of a noble spirit." He adds, with a glance at himself, " The man that God has touched is always a being apart." And so he would fain give hospitality to this wandering soul, whose thoughts, however, had been " too simple to be true."

Professing German ideas in a mere literary Paris, opposed to the ways of the University,

and claiming the right of private judgment under Napoleon III, who was nervously anxious to
keep on terms with St. Michael, while not putting
down Satan too violently, it was clear that Renan
would raise up foes on every side. To J. J. Weiss,
who wanted such a quarrel, Taine wrote in January, 1858, " I regret what you say about Renan.
I know him personally; I own that his hands are
too ecclesiastically gloved; but he is very eager,
attached to his convictions, immensely learned, rich
in general ideas; he has the refinement of an artist
and a man of the world; he will be one of the
great men of this century." Others divined his
coming influence. Augustin Thierry, to whose
place in the Academy of Inscriptions Renan succeeded in 1856, and who died a Catholic, had
taught him how facts might be made interesting
and historical periods set out in bold relief. M.
de Sacy, an old-world Jansenist, treated him as a
favorite pupil, when they met at the office of the
Journal des Débats, where Renan exercised his
pen with effect in the cause of freedom. For he
was a Liberal, as Englishmen construe the word,
though he felt some hankerings after protection
for those frail objects, art and literature, which
the crowd is only too apt to trample down in its
march.

His home life was exceedingly happy. Henriette and Cornélie vied in devotion to him. He lost a little daughter, Ernestine; but his boy, Ary, who figures in the correspondence as Bébé, lived to be a poet and draughtsman of promising skill. His mother had now given up Tréguier. She was living under the same roof with her children in the Val de Grace, and resigned herself (somewhat as Carlyle's mother in circumstances not unlike) to the ways of a son who assured her that his religion was at heart the worship of Jesus. She could not but feel elated as he grew famous in so brilliant a sphere. Full of spirit, herself a woman of great natural endowments, she softened Henriette's austerity and brought out the livelier gifts of her daughter-in-law.

M. Ary Scheffer died in 1858. But another death had occurred, several months previously, on which the future of Renan, his wife, and his sister, was to depend. M. de Quatremère had expired in September, 1857, leaving the chair of Hebrew vacant in the Collège de France. It was a position that his most distinguished pupil meant to inherit. But how would public opinion regard the authorities who should put the Bible, as it were officially, into Renan's hands? To ask for it was like throwing down a gage of battle. " I cannot, however," he wrote to Berthelot, " accept for myself or for science the part of *capitis minor.*" He appeared as a candidate; the engagement was begun.

Renan's apology for his act will be quoted in due course. But we may say at once that the Collège de France was never, it would seem, an ecclesiastical institution; and, though at Oxford Pusey insisted on teaching Hebrew as a part of divinity, this view could scarcely find favor with a mere critic. " Independent science " was the cry on one side; " respect for the established religion of Frenchmen," was retorted on the other. Some of the less wise declared that Renan was ignorant of Hebrew. He answered by publishing a remarkable translation of the Book of Job, and an ingenious, if too fanciful, dramatic interpretation of Solomon's Song. There could be no doubt that he was qualified to fill a chair of Semitic languages; whether in that chair he might express himself freely concerning the Sacred Scriptures was a question of propriety and public order. The nomination did not take place at this time. A substitute was appointed, and Renan still maintained his candidature. He would offer no compromise. The Emperor, whose religious indifference was absolute, looked round for a distinction which he might bestow on this unconquered Liberal. The French troops were about to occupy the Lebanon, as in 1849 they had occupied Rome. Napoleon offered him a mission in search of Phœnician antiquities, not very largely endowed, and, on Henriette's advice, he accepted the charge. His sister made up her mind to go with him. Ary was to be left at home; Cornélie might follow her husband afterward. Berthelot saw his two friends off at Marseilles, where they embarked for Beyrout in a French transport on October 21, 1860.

CHAPTER IV

GALILEE AND AFTERWARD

From this voyage Henriette was never to return. Her brother's absorption in his work grew daily. He had ceased to be a lively correspondent, as in his Italian tour; the pains which he spent on authorship forbade it. All his mind was given to that daring enterprise which shone through the Syrian expedition and above it like a star. In his *Future of Science* we observed the prophetic words which announced that the greatest book of the nineteenth century would be entitled, *The Critical History of the Christian Origins*. Even now the image of a human and ideal Jesus of Nazareth, filled his imagination. He was not destined to bring back from Tyre and Sidon much that an archæologist would value. But the landscape of Galilee, the Syrian sky, the beauty of Hermon and Lebanon—these were to be his great discoveries. And for them Henriette paid with her life—no reluctant victim.

They reached Beyrout in the early days of November, 1860. "If you would set eyes on the

strangest mixture of things charming and hideous," Renan wrote to his friend, " a natural scen-
ery of which the grace is beyond words, an incomparable sky, a sea that is a wonder, the finest
mountains, the filthiest cities, a horrible race not
wanting in exquisite types, and society in the lowest stage, come out hither."   Lebanon intoxicated
him.   These smiling Alps were the paradise of
God.   His magnificent health, in which he put too
much confidence, and this delightful season, urged
him to labor and to move about incessantly, accompanied by his sister when possible, bent as he
was on finding inscriptions and monuments by day,
and at night busy with his writing.   They took
up their regular quarters at Amschit, not far from
the ancient Byblos, lodging with a wealthy Maronite, Zakhia, in a pleasant house which overlooked
the sea.

Berthelot had just brought out the work on
synthetic chemistry, which Renan called his *Pro-
pylæa*.   It was a success, and to the explorer a
challenge.   It spurred him to activity; while his
anxious friend talked of Syrian fever, and Henriette mourned over a selfish devotion to art which
seemed to kill affection, the days passed.   Cornélie, it was decided, should join them at once;
Berthelot projected an expedition also, but could
never manage it.   If any words might persuade

him, Renan's description of ruined Maschnaka would have succeeded. "It is the valley of Adonis," he said, "if we may term that a valley which is a precipice more than a thousand feet down, the space between no more than a few hundred. There begin the lasting snows of winter. On the horizon, the white domes of Aphaca. The contrast of snowy wind and brilliant sun is indescribable. Two glaciers, not large, in two sunless hollows, are enchanting." The valley of the river Adonis appeared in his eyes the most ravishing sight he had ever seen. "One can fancy nothing more romantic or more solemn. It is a landscape made for lamentation over the dead gods." At no great distance from this place Henriette was to find a tomb.

Her first illness occurred in February, 1861. Of her brother she wrote that he was no longer the same, he was quite transformed. Berthelot, deeply troubled, begged them both to return. "I believe your sister is always ill," he insisted; "let her come back." Ernest, however, would not hearken. He went on with his excavations at Tyre, after which they set out for Galilee and Jerusalem, arriving in May at the Holy City. Thirty-four days, never to be forgotten by him, were spent in Palestine, and at the end of July Cornélie quitted her husband. She was expecting the birth of another child. Henriette should now have gone home. The French army, suffering from fever, were leaving Syria. But she lingered, though terribly fatigued, while Ernest, at Ghazir on the slopes of Lebanon, was flinging down on paper as fast as he could, with happy eagerness, his vision of the "gentle Galilean." From Beyrout he announced triumphantly to Berthelot, on September 12, 1861, "In eight days it will be finished." Not pale phantoms or abstract types, he said, but living figures—such were to be his creations. "This great fragment in my portfolio is all my strength," he declared, but it must not be advertised too soon. His friend answered on September 26, "Your letter breathes I know not what secret joy." Two days earlier Henriette had passed away at Amschit.

The last rites were given to her by a good Maronite priest while her brother was lying unconscious in a fever-dream. He had not fancied her indisposition serious; and he was busy embarking his monuments at Beyrout, when, on returning to Amschit, the burning sun struck him down. Except for one or two passing moments, he did not know what had befallen himself or his beloved sister. She had spoken to him about her last will; he was to have all she might leave. Her thoughts dwelt on the friends at home; and she excused her jealous affection for him by saying, " Je t'ai aimé comme on n'aime plus." On the Tuesday, at three in the morning, she died. Zakhia opened his father's tomb, and in it she found a resting-place, hard by a chapel under the palm-trees. " There let her wait for me," wrote Ernest, in after-days, " beneath the palms of Amschit, in the land of ancient mysteries, nigh unto sacred By-blos." . . .

Alone, hardly recovered, and with a deepening sense of what he had lost, Renan came back to the Academy of Inscriptions and to the world of Paris. Taine writes to Édouard de Suckau on February 8, 1862, " Renan is returned from the East as cross as an owl; Berthelot is worn out." A super-ficial judgment; in that sturdy constitution of the returned pilgrim, there was obstinacy, but not ill-humor. He was now meditating the boldest act of the nineteenth century. That act would be a memorial of the unknown Henriette, whose legacy to her brother, as he often said, was the *Life of Jesus*. During the pleasant sojourn at Ghazir it had been thrown off in the white heat of inspira-tion, kindled by their journey together as they went up from Galilee to Jerusalem and rode back again to Lebanon. " Delightful hours, too quickly van-ished! " he cried, when she was no more. " Ah, may Eternity be like them! From morning till night I was drunk with the thought that unrolled itself before me.   I fell asleep upon it, and the first ray of dawn behind the mountain gave it back to me clearer and more living than the eve.   Henriette watched the growth of my work day by day; when I had finished a page, it was hers to copy it. In the evening we walked on our terrace under the brilliant stars; she offered me her thoughts, remarkable for their tact and insight, some of which came to me as a revelation.   Her joy was full; those moments, doubtless, were the sweetest in her life."

There is, commonly, in great crises, a union of the many elements which make for drama.   Renan's whole soul was concentrated on his manuscript, the publication of which would stir all France and might be his ruin, when he found himself gazetted, on January 11, 1862, to the chair of Hebrew.   The two Academies had sent up his name on request of the Minister.   Napoleon III appointed him, and a storm of protest at once broke out.

Oriental scholars, it would appear, did not believe that a man who wrote such exquisite French could be pedantic enough for the teaching of dead literatures.   Young men in the Latin Quarter set down the Liberal who had taken the Emperor's bribe as a renegade.   Catholics declared the nom-

ination an insult to their faith. And Renan himself, who never answered critics, but whose nerves
were in good order, welcomed, though he did not
show any indiscreet exultation, the tumult which
brought him before all men's eyes. It was the
path to glory which he had long been expecting
to see open. Friends advised him to begin his
course on a special subject, in the hall where his
predecessor had lectured to half-a-dozen students.
His answer was that he would do so by and by.
First, he had resolved to speak on his general
duties as a teacher, in the large amphitheatre of
the Collège de France.

The day came, February 21, 1862. Outside,
the crowd was so violent that the police had to
clear the courtyard by force; within, the great
spaces were occupied by opposing and opposed
battalions, orthodox, freethinking, revolutionary.
Renan was greeted with hisses and applause. But
for twenty minutes he could not obtain a hearing.
His written discourse was read, however, at length,
amid the cheers and counter-cheers which broke it
into fragments. The subject in itself was worthy
of philosophic handling. "What part have the
Semites contributed to Western civilization?" Renan inquired. "They have brought us religion,"
he answered; "to them we are indebted for the
most extraordinary of moral events that have

changed the world." Everyone caught the allusion; freethinkers applauded, Christians turned
pale with excitement. The speaker did not pause;
but his words floated uncertain over the gathering
storm. "An incomparable man," he continued,
reading from his notes, "so great that, although
we must judge of all things in this place from the
view of positive science, I would not gainsay those
who, struck by the exceptional character of his
work, have called him God—he it was that established the everlasting religion of humanity, the
religion of the spirit." But he went on to say,
"the high thought of Jesus, scarcely understood
by His disciples, has undergone many defeats,"
and "in adopting Christianity, we have profoundly altered it; in reality, it is our creation."

By this time all was a sea of raging sounds.
The young Liberals cheered; their opponents cried
out at this blasphemer. Taine, who was present,
remarked afterward that the orator's action was
"somewhat episcopal—a bishop *in partibus infi-
delium,*" and so were certain phrases of his lecture. "He is too unctuous," concluded the severe
Hegelian. But an unction which breaks the head
is more exasperating than a quarter-staff. The
Catholic young men could not forgive him. To
the freethinkers it was a glorious day; they "applauded coarsely," says Taine once more, "like

readers of the *Siècle*," and forming a procession of umbrellas—it was raining hard—they went off to the Rue Madame and cheered under the new professor's windows. He had escaped from the amphitheatre by a side exit. The irony of circumstances was complete when Madame Veuve Renan, Catholic and orthodox, came out above, to receive congratulations from this noisy crowd of unbelievers on behalf of her son.

Next day, the lectures were suspended by Government. They were said to threaten public order. But Renan would not resign. For two years he went on accepting the emoluments of his chair, and teaching Hebrew to all who would attend his lessons. The Emperor could not send him a *lettre de cachet,* and there was no Bastille. On the other hand, superior persons smiled at the "menace to public order" which a company of gendarmes might have dealt with safely. Yet the question in Paris, which is the city of heat as well as of light, was more serious than it would have seemed in any other European capital. When the Bible was discussed on platforms, and an official person, almost one of the Government, as French opinion held and still holds in all such cases, could openly set down Jesus Christ on the level of mere humanity, there was danger in the air. Mr. Stuart Mill, no enemy to freedom of thought and speech, has told us that " undoubtedly the manner of asserting an opinion, even though it be a true one, may be very objectionable, and may justly incur severe censure." We might ask, also, what science could hope to gain by Renan's lecture, in presence of a chance assembly, the purpose of which was not to learn anything, but to manifest its like or dislike of the heterodox professor? He was now doing, under provocation if we will, the very thing which he had charged upon Victor Cousin as undignified. Was he not degrading his erudition to politics? His friends have, in effect, granted so much. But the overpowering sense of his " great fragment," now secure in his portfolio, drove him on like a goad. He yearned for the battle that could not long be delayed, the thunder of the captains and the shouting.

In 1847 he had written from Tréguier to his fellow-student, that Christianity was " dead and well dead "; that nothing could be made of it unless it were transformed; and that he perceived in their own century the elements of a new religion. This latter hope had waned. But his ideal system might still wear a halo, if it could be shown that Jesus of Nazareth was its supreme expression. Certainly, Renan was willing to make converts; the hour of disappointment had not sounded in his ears. To his colleagues he now addressed a mani-

festo, defending his inaugural lecture, on which
we shall have more to say by and by. It ended
with a defiant prophecy that, if silenced in his
chair, he could still publish books and find an audience who would listen to him. The allusion was
transparent. And on June 23, 1863, *The Life
of Jesus* appeared.

Its success was immediate, far-reaching, and
extraordinary. In November sixty-five thousand
copies had been sold. But that was only a symptom of the universal interest. On all sides men
looked upon the volume as a banner lifted up,
which must be attacked or defended. In the eyes
of Catholics it was a crime without parallel, an
offence against God and man. The fierce assault
which they at once opened upon it made *The Life
of Jesus* known to every priest in France. Not a
clerical meeting was held between Provence and
Brittany but its demerits came up for discussion.
Abroad, it leaped into fame at a bound. French
was now, as it long had been, the common language of society and of culture. Such a book,
appearing in English, would have taken five years
to cross the Channel. To England, Bishop Co-
lenso was the critic who gave offence, but who
could not win renown, by his dull cross-examining
of the numbers in the Pentateuch. Strauss had

put forward his theory, which resolved the Four
Gospels into myth and allegory, a generation earlier. But to the frivolous coteries of Paris that
German professor was only a name; and not so
much as a name to the French clergy at large.
What, then, had Renan achieved? Something
great, if not portentous. Thanks to his unrivalled
command of language, to the color of his description, to the suavity of a sentimentalism which enchanted without rhetoric, he had transformed the
Gospels into a publication of the day. Dealing
with pages hitherto regarded as the Latin of the
Mass, which only priests recited, while none but
the faithful listened, he made of them a French
classic, and the least orthodox now read with surprise how beautiful they could be.

Not for a moment did this latest of New Testa-
ments, thus boldly thrown upon the ways of men,
prevail because it was learned, or exact, or creative
as high poetry may be when it takes up realities
from the past. Renan has keenly observed that
French literature, since the time of Louis XIII,
is a tertiary formation; it is Greek rendered into
Latin, and this again manipulated by Racine or
Molière, to suit the people of the Seine. In like
manner his own most venturesome book, though
not his greatest, gives back the Hebrew strength
and sweetness which so marvellously work upon

us in the Gospels, not as he finds them there, but qualified to please a literary taste. His version stands to St. Matthew or St. Luke much as *Télé-maque* stands to the *Iliad* and the *Odyssey*. A man of letters who had quarrelled with Renan, Edmond de Goncourt, called it the Bible *féne-lonisé,* and so far justly, that from the " swan of Cambray " its author had learned the secret of " painting by moral strokes," on which he prided himself. The " Hebrew truth," to speak with St. Jerome, had been softened down into an idyl, which was not truly Eastern, but which corre-sponded to the decadent mood of *Paul and Vir-ginia,* and was sometimes more than a little cloying in its over-sweetness.

For that effect several reasons may be assigned. Renan had never passed through the fire of a pas-sion that cleanses and heightens emotion. Though the son of many prophets, he was no prophet him-self. His art is delicate rather than sublime; and of French sentiment the danger has always been a pretty affectation tending toward the madrigal. Again, he could not, like the true magician, shoot his soul into another form and there be something different from what he was by nature. He drew portraits by looking in the glass. He stays with his readers and in front of them, hinting how like the picture is to the painter by subtle asides and a knowing smile.   Without books, having only Josephus and the Greek New Testament at hand, dreaming open-eyed in divine Galilee, the Breton fancied how things might have seemed to him, had he been among the disciples, on the Lake of Gennesareth, or as they went through the Sabbath fields, and plucked the ripe ears of corn.   That which was instantly admired, and which alone will not be forgotten, in the *Life of Jesus,* was the Galilean episode.   The landscape gave birth to the character, not any well-interpreted documents. But again, the character may be traced in Renan's own history with its varying stages; Brittany is the key to Nazareth, Paris shadows forth Jerusalem.   By " gently soliciting " the inspired text, as he admitted, or, says M. Séailles, by arbitrary cuttings in it according as they suited his purpose, Renan put together, in mosaic fashion, a sentimental romance which was colored from end to end by his own experience.

By divination, therefore, and by conjecture, as he tells us at the outset, was a task so formidable to be fulfilled.   Not that Renan considered it beyond his powers.   He said in after-years, " I am the one man of my century that has understood Jesus and St. Francis of Assisi."   The sketch of that " Umbrian Christ," which he had already attempted, was a prelude to this supreme endeavor.

Yet neither sketch nor masterpiece can be judged a triumph before the only court to which, in his *Future of Science,* the author would have appealed. For the facts do not lead up, as they ought, to the explanation; but, contrariwise, Renan starts with an axiom *a priori* before which the documents give way. He breaks up the unity of a living spirit when he divides between the legend and the truth, rejects the miraculous, and, however more exquisitely than Voltaire, yet on the same principles, brings down the life of Saint or Saviour to a moral apologue.

These are not merely the views of orthodox Christians. Strauss had resolved the Gospels into a myth, no part of which could be verified, because he felt that they must be taken or left as a whole. George Eliot, his translator, shared that opinion. She writes, slightly in Mr. Casaubon's vein, " For minds acquainted with the European culture of the last half-century, Renan's book can furnish no new result; and they are likely to set little store by the too facile construction of a life from materials of which the biographical significance becomes more dubious as they are more closely examined." She would not, however, cast utterly away the " Idea of Christ "; she believed in a " sacred past of one woof with the human present." Renan might have echoed these last words; but, if he had no facts to go upon, his volume was simply a mixture from the painter's palette. Science, in that event, would pass by on the other side. Or, again to quote George Eliot, "this *Vie de Jésus,* and still more, Renan's *Letter to Berthelot,* have compelled me to give up the high estimate I had formed of his mind." Artistic merit he certainly did possess; but he was not, as she had reckoned him, among the finest thinkers of the time.

If such was the verdict uttered by one who marched in the vanguard toward that "new religion" called of Humanity, we may expect from others, like Carlyle, who thought history should deal with what had really happened, a more emphatic condemnation. Carlyle disliked the book, and wished it had not been written. On the minds of German scholars, believing as Tholuck, or sceptical as the later Strauss, it left no trace discernible. "Das ist nichts," said Tholuck, many days afterward, to an American inquirer. Ewald and Keim were severe upon this romance, "which professed to deal with great questions, but which answered none." And though Renan protested against such criticism, it was only an exception when Mommsen declared him to be "a savant, in spite of his beautiful style." Tübingen was yet in the ascendant—a school "without tact or measure," said the French writer almost bitterly,

which carried its denials too far. But, we may
rejoin, was he not himself imaginative beyond the
letter of his documents? "The striking agree-
ment of texts and situations, the wonderful con-
cord between the evangelical idea and the country
that served as its frame," might be an argument
when we had evidence to bear it up; and it had
come to the traveller as a revelation. Yet, surely,
taken for the ground of faith, topography was
not enough. To students, as to believers, Renan
brought no message. How, then, did he fare with
his own French public, in the " diocese of Sainte
Beuve," as it was wittily termed, where he pontifi-
cated rather more than to austere freethinkers like
Taine was pleasing?

At first, loud and triumphant was their acclaim.
That which scandalized Christians gave them matter of exultation. In the struggle for life and
death between Catholics and infidels, one Name
had, as by tacit consent, been respected. True,
there was a literature for the lower classes which
went to every length; but hitherto, in chairs such
as Renan occupied, and in serious writings, the
Gospels were treated with decorum. A new thing
had come to pass. When the Romans besieged an
enemy's city, they called on its tutelar gods to leave
it and follow them to the Capitol. This unhappy
fugitive from the Christian altar was busy with a

like incantation. He desired to make the Prophet of Nazareth an idealist who had set him the example, a free spirit in revolt against the hierarchy. The cause of Jesus was to be severed from that of the Church and to be identified with revolution. Who should seize this flag was now the question. A merely human Jesus would be ruin to all possible creeds which rested on faith in God. That was, undoubtedly, the issue at stake; and however little prepared for so fresh a problem, Catholics like Meignan, afterward bishop and cardinal of Tours, saw what they had to encounter. The supernatural would be vanquished if Jesus were left in His enemies' keeping.

But rebels have never known how to deal with a captive king, except to make away with him, and so it proved now. Renan, in spite of his art, which is especially cunning in its juxtaposition of elements not by nature agreeing, fills the canvas with cloud when what we are seeking is light. He cannot explain the miraculous. His wavering policy reduces it to legend, misunderstanding, illusion, innocent deceit; all subterfuges of his own temperament, which was curiously insensible to the abnormal, and, on this side, was not less frigid than Hume's. Renan felt uneasy when he heard men talk of Providence; the touch of a Divine Hand made him shiver. He meant as decidedly as any

Rationalist to clear away the inexplicable in which the Gospels abound. Then the dilemma returns —were those miracles a concession to credulity, or were they sincerely wrought? Choose either alternative, but abide by the consequences. A miracle-working teacher would be fatal to Renan's scientific principles; a Jesus who was not sincere, though but a reluctant impostor, would be no pattern for men to live by. Under the double strain, this new construction falls to pieces. We grasp in it no distinct figure, and that which, by design, was to be the grandest of all literary creations, melts into mist and shadow beyond the domain of history when we compare it to the Gospels.

In a sentence that drew smiles, Renan has likened himself to the " fabulous beast of Ctesias," one half of which devours the other half. Contradiction he gloried in, when his own reasoning led up to it, as a sign that he saw all round the object. He said also that " the real is a vast outrage on the ideal." Nevertheless, it is wisely observed that we must know the life of Hamlet before we can invent a theory of Hamlet. The application is immediate. What did Renan mean by history when he called it to M. Berthelot his " reason "? If not facts that had taken place, and men that had thought and wrought them, could it be other than an idle dream? To this note of

Madame Ernest Renan.
From a painting by Ary Scheffer

interrogation his answer is, "What you will."
He cannot be sure, as we have seen repeatedly,
whether he criticizes dogma because it is impossible, or because it may be convicted of falsehood.
Sometimes his argument runs, "Every alleged
miracle is a legend"; but again he lets that fall
to insist on discrepancies in the evidence. He is
realist and idealist by turns. The illuminating
vision of a Thucydides, the insight of a Shakespeare when moving over the stage of time, he
never had.

It is significant that, whether dealing with Old
Testament or New, not a hint drops from his pen
which has proved fertile of undiscovered truths
regarding either. He waits upon the Germans,
Baur or Strauss or Wellhausen, from whose conjectures he may glean for his poetry of the Bible.
He has cleared up no difficulties, started no in-
vestigations, fixed no disputable points of custom
or language. His contribution to the Gospel is
a dissolving view where the hallucinated writer
infects with his fancies a reader who is taken by
delightful words. His sympathies even for the
highest are intermittent. He loves the Jesus of
Galilee; when the last days come at Jerusalem and
a tragic note is sounded, too deep for his calm
temper, he hesitates, is bewildered, and turns from
the scene. He cannot endure a crucified Christ,

or allow any substance to a risen one. The glory
of Jesus, he affirms, does not consist in His being
relegated beyond history; a true devotion will show
that all history is incomprehensible without Him.
Yet this "capital event in the world's record,"
unique as it is confessed to be, our fifth evangelist
leaves unresolved into its only adequate causes.
For neither Christian nor antichristian has accepted the phantom, which is all that Renan pre-
sents to them as an historical reality.

In truth, we cannot, to please George Eliot or
any of her school, divide "the idea of Christ"
from "the man Jesus." As well might we attempt to understand Christianity itself, without
following back its pedigree in Israel to the Hebrew prophets. But Renan, by appealing at one
time to the pure idea and at another to the Gospel
story, on no fixed principle of which we can take
account, has evaporated into ether that supreme
personality which is the incarnation of both.

It has been lately said of Renan's *Life of Jesus*
that it is "by far the most subtle attempt ever
made to deprive Christ of His divine attributes,
and reduce Him to the level of a mere philosopher
or dreamer." So much may be granted, and no
manipulation of epithets, designedly vague, will
restore the true lineaments on a canvas like this,
the ground-tone of which is mere Nature. On the

other hand, from a scandal so arresting, and of such proportions, which has been perpetuated in thirty-three editions at home, with translations and cheap issues in every European language, one result, hardly anticipated by its author, is becoming daily more evident. The *Life of Christ,* passing from technical theology, from catechisms and sermons, into literature, vindicates to itself an importance as the first in every sense of human biographies, and the centre of history. Between sacred and profane the old wall of division has been broken down. It is impossible for any man to explain the world without fixing his regard on Jesus. He is real to the present generation, even of those who do not believe, as He never was to the Voltairian or the freethinker of a previous age. Theologians comprehend, in a more vivid fashion than ever before, that creeds and dogmas are but aspects of His words, His works, His personality. Critics know that they have to deal with Him as a fact. And the relation of Church and Testament is explored on all sides, with a view to discovering the Founder in the institution, and to bring out His truth in the record.

No " Life," indeed, undertaken by a modern, is likely to satisfy the demands both of critical science and of vital religion; yet none, perhaps, has been entirely a failure. Of Renan's own it must be allowed that the Galilean pages are often exquisite as landscape, or setting, or embroidery on a theme which was constantly too great for him. If we take his point of view, the everlasting splendor of Deity fades from that countenance; but there is left a simple yet profound sense of joy in this renewal of the world's youth, amid a flowering Paradise, where the disciples troop about their Master, and He awakens in them all the qualities that were soon to be called Christian—humility, faith, detachment, an eager looking for the Kingdom of God. It is a pastoral play over which floats the music of the Beatitudes; a story that runs into parables and delights in imagery caught from the life around, from lake and field, springtide and harvest, while the fierce hubbub of an unregenerate world sounds only as a murmur afar off. All this Renan touches with a pencil the effect of which is often something too soft; we are put in mind of the Caracci; but he succeeds admirably in what Catholic writers term the " composition of place," or the framework for devout meditation.

He is, of course, not equal to the loftier task of delineating character. At no time has he set before us any other than his own. Trained in the seminary to abstract reasoning, brought up on texts and analysis, busy with small points of criticism, and not very observant of life as he went his way, the student could never be a creator. He is not direct enough in his strokes, nor can he deliver them with force and sharpness enough, to fix on our memories a clear outline. We should never have known Jesus or His chosen followers, had we to learn our Gospel for the first time in these chapters, which engage us while we read them, but which melt into a summer-cloud when we have laid the book aside.

Though by temper sceptical, Renan was not disposed to follow his German guides to their extreme conclusions. When he has to tell of the last scenes at Jerusalem, he quotes the Gospel of St. John as, to a large extent, authentic; he accepts the episode of Bethany more or less from his hands; the discourses, we are told, cannot be relied upon, but the facts were familiar to the Fourth Evangelist. A position so conservative roused up the younger Teutons; and in later editions Renan yielded somewhat under their attack. But he maintained always that, however perplexing the Johannine problem might be, there was no reasonable ground for dissociating the Apostle from a work which embodied his reminiscences. And he thought a more moderate view would tone down the " rigor and vigor," as Matthew Arnold termed it, of Baur's absolute denials. This, thanks to fresh documents

and a less airy method, has actually come to pass.
Arnold himself, though no great authority as regards evidence, was much too fine a critic not to
perceive that in the themes of the Fourth Gospel
a kinship may be established with what we possess
in the other three. If, as Renan is never tired
of repeating, Jesus " was more than the reformer
of an old religion," if He created " the everlasting
religion of humanity," then His assertions about
Himself in St. John are inevitable echoes of words
uttered in the vehement disputes at Jerusalem
which led up to the end. He who declared Himself to be the Messiah, could not but claim the
powers and attributes of which those discourses
are so emphatic in their ascription to Him. Such
claims are already visible in the Synoptics; and
nothing else would suffice to account for the
charges on which Jesus was condemned to death
by the Jewish Sanhedrim.

Our Gospels take us on to the Resurrection.
But Renan pauses when Calvary is reached. For
him the Son of Man now enters into the ideal,
which becomes a kind of immortality. He ad-
dresses Christ on the cross in terms of passionate
recognition. " Thou," he exclaims, " art destined
to become the corner-stone of Humanity in such
wise that to tear Thy name from this world, would
be to shake it to its foundations." And he con-

cludes by saying that " whatever be the unexpected events of the future, Jesus will never be surpassed. His worship will renew its youth unceasingly; his legend will call forth tears without end; his sufferings will touch the best of hearts; all ages will proclaim that among the sons of men a greater was never born than Jesus."

CHAPTER V

IN ST. PAUL'S FOOTSTEPS

WHILE his book was making such a stir, Renan with his family had been enjoying a summer expedition to Dinard, from which they went on, in August, 1863, to Jersey. He had resolved not to answer his critics; but he wrote, not quite in his usual temper, to a Scottish friend, Mr. (now Sir Mountstuart) Grant Duff, " Sometimes, I confess, when I observe the rage that my volume has provoked among the orthodox, I almost repent of having published it. I did not expect so much passion or party spirit. However, what I have done was in absolute sincerity." His friend Berthelot, not many days later, told him, " When you come back, you will not be merely assailed with small troubles; look out for a storm of contradiction and hatred:—pope, archbishops, bishops, curés, deacons and subdeacons, not to speak of the third order and the sons of ex-Liberals. But you will get the upper hand of all that by holding to your opinions; Voltaire stood out well, without much persecution. But you are in for it as long as you live; and you will escape persecution simply if you never flinch. Your name will be conspicuous in the nineteenth century, as the *philosophers* were in the eighteenth. The insistence and lasting hatred of Catholics will suffice to point out your way."

Berthelot added that the Empress Eugénie, who of course did not share Renan's views, defended his freedom as a writer; but that neither friend nor foe expected the resumption of his lectures at the Collège de France. The lecturer was not daunted. He might be deprived of his chair, but the public would buy and read him; a strong body of opinion, which had its centre in Paris, would back him up. M. Taschereau had offered him a position as Under-Keeper of MSS. in the Imperial Library, where he was formerly an assistant, with seven thousand francs a year; but he could not hold it and continue to be professor of Hebrew. He had answered by a distinct refusal on that very ground. He thought of demanding from M. Duruy permission to open a " free course "; if that were not allowed, he would come forward as a Parliamentary candidate for Paris. Berthelot, who was in close relations with Government, replied to his friend that the Emperor minded very little about the lectures in themselves, but it was a question of public order, and they would inevitably lead to disturbance. "France," he said, "is in no condition to hear scientific truth without passion one way or the other; I am not sure that other countries would be more patient under the circumstances in which you announce it, and which are not those of abstract erudition." Renan's work had been great and successful; but reaction could not be avoided. The *Life of Jesus* was not a *Life of Buddha;* it implied "an action of propaganda," which the other did not. Far from being engaged in pure science, Renan found himself in the midst of battle. So judged his most intimate acquaintance; and we ought not to overlook that judgment when the champion of unbelief deprecates, as we have seen, the rage of party spirit that had been stirred up against him. Had he not stirred it up himself?

The rest of the story is soon told. In July, 1862, the professor, on being silenced, had addressed to his colleagues a letter which was much more of an explanation than an apology, as regarded his inaugural lecture. He pleaded for perfect freedom as a scientific man to express whatever he thought to be true, provided his language was respectful toward the object of it and kept clear of religious controversy. There had never existed in the Collège de France a chair of divinity proper. That lay institution, founded by

Francis I, aimed at learning rather than teaching; it investigated and explored. What Renan himself intended was a course of Hebrew literature as such; and if he had drawn upon general considerations in beginning it, he did but follow the ordinary custom. For his method he appealed to Reuchlin, Henri Étienne and Descartes, who were scholars but did not pretend to be theologians; as for the condition which determined his handling of the Bible, that also was scientific, namely, the exclusion of miracles or the supernatural from all arguments which dealt with facts. And he proceeded to quote M. Littré, the Positivist, whose words to this effect were constantly on his lips. But to separate religion from the supernatural was not to be irreligious. The notion of miracles was a lost cause. He ended by saying that he would not be stopped by anyone and that he could wait. If to-day ten people would not listen while he spoke, to-morrow ten thousand would read what he had written. In 1863 his prophecy had been more than fulfilled; but he was not to lecture again in the chair of Hebrew for many years.

His Liberal friends were now anxious that he should come out as a candidate in Paris for the Corps Législatif. But in face of a strong opposition, Conservative as well as Catholic, he had no chance. It is difficult to imagine Renan as a popular chief; he was better guided by instinct when he turned his back on the insignificant party-strifes of the next few years, and visited the cradle-lands of Christianity once more. In November, 1864, he arrived at Alexandria on his way to the East. By this time his quarrel with Government had passed into the fifth and last act. On June 2 the world had been informed, by means of an official report in the *Moniteur,* that a new chair of Comparative Philology would absorb the funds previously allocated to the chair of Hebrew. But by way of compensation, M. Renan was named Assistant-Keeper of MSS.—an offer which he had rejected nine months earlier.

That very day he sent to the Minister of Education a polite but scathing letter, declining the functions thrust upon him, and firm in his contention that he had never been deprived of his post. He had not given up teaching; as for the stipend which was paid him, "science," he said, "takes into account the results achieved, not the carrying out more or less punctually of a regulation; if, M. le Ministre, you ever make it a reproach that the scientific man who does honor to his country has not earned the poor allowance which the State doles out to him, believe me, he will answer you as I do at this moment, and after an illustrious example, ' Pecunia tua tecum sit.'

Apply then, M. le Ministre, the funds voted for the chair of Hebrew, Chaldee, and Syriac to any purpose you think proper. I shall keep the title which I owe to the double presentation of the professors in the Collège de France and my colleagues at the Institute. Without a stipend I will discharge the duties laid on me by that title, and do my utmost to promote the studies intrusted to my keeping."

This challenge was answered by a fresh decree signed " Napoleon," in the *Moniteur* of June 12, which cancelled Renan's appointment to the Imperial Library, and relieved him of his duties in the Collège de France. No reasons were given. But everyone recognized that, after the *Vie de Jésus* had taken its place among European books as an event of the first magnitude, its author could not hope to escape reprisals in a country where, as he said, all questions ran into politics. Until the Second Empire fell, Renan was in opposition to the Government, though he became an intimate friend of some among the Bonapartes. He greatly admired Prince Jerome Napoleon; he was on familiar terms, as a frequent guest, with the Princess Mathilde, whose genius he rated very high, and whose drawing-room at St. Gratien was a centre of artistic and literary meetings. Before 1863 Renan might have claimed the reputation of a scholar among scholars; the French public did not know him. From that climacteric year of the nineteenth century, which proved, thanks to the Mexican adventure, to be a fatal one for the House of Bonaparte, his renown went on increasing.

He was just turned forty. His character had not lost its firmness; he meditated volumes more solid and erudite than the unsubstantial romance by which he had achieved a doubtful fame as the Celsus of a new Paganism, loftily patronizing what believers adored. Antiquity was his subject, sunshine his element. On his first expedition to Palestine he went as a poet; from his second he came back an historian, always indeed mixing his own dreams with realities, but writing over again the Roman annals where they touched the Christian in a style no less delicate than persuasive. Yet on these delightful undertakings events of the darkest tragedy were to cast their shadow.

From Alexandria, which he found " dirty, hideous, vulgar, disgusting in its immorality, baseness, and deformity," Renan wrote in November, 1864, to Berthelot that he was on his way to Cairo and the Pyramids. All he intended was a flying visit; but M. Mariette, who directed the French excavations—a man of rare charm and scholarship—led him along the Nile for five hundred miles, as far

as the First Cataract. He suffered a little from
sunstroke at Thebes, but was otherwise in excellent
health and spirits, eager to see everything like an
indefatigable tourist, and sending to the *Journal
des Débats* an account of it all, which is still pleasant reading.

He was infinitely curious about the ancient
world. Its greatness never failed to carry him
away; for, like Newman, he did not believe it had
been surpassed by later civilizations. Henceforth,
more than ever, his tone is that of a Greek, nay,
an Athenian who composes in French because the
Attic idiom would find no readers, and who among
his modern acquaintance is a survival from the age
of Pericles. Well as he understood Hebrew, the
attitude in which he drew nigh to Prophet or Apostle was by no means sympathetic. Their burning
enthusiasm repelled him; so vehement a style he
could not away with; he thought them even a little
wanting in good manners. Such was the frame
of mind in which Renan set forth to trace the life
and journeyings of St. Paul.

Madame Renan went with her husband, who
could not bear to travel by himself. The children,
Ary and Noemi, were left at home. From Beyrout, in a January which might have been April,
the pilgrims rode through anemones and cycla-
mens on their " sweet sad expedition " to Amschit,

where Henriette lay buried. They were welcomed by patriarch and people with open arms.

The tomb was on a slope of Lebanon, between two valleys from which the sea was visible, and the port of Byblos, encumbered with ruins, toward the south. All round about flourished vines, olive-groves, and palms, while the mountains which closed in the horizon were covered with snow. Renan had thought of giving his beloved sister a separate grave and of raising a monument over it. But Zakhia the Maronite pleaded hard that she might rest in the sepulchre of his family, and so it was determined. In the chapel not far off, at Renan's petition, Mass was celebrated according to that ancient Syrian rite, the whole village joining in. "This for me is now holy ground," he wrote to Berthelot; "I shall come back again; I have left there one of the best parts of myself." Only those who compare the Epicurean of his latter years with Henriette's brother as he was during her lifetime, will measure how truly he spoke.

Damascus, "melancholy and sombre," was the next stage. "I have fixed my horizon," he wrote again to his friend in Paris, "for the scene of St. Paul's conversion. It came to pass in a great cultivated plain, perhaps in the midst of gardens. We must certainly put aside the notion of an outward accident; the whole thing took place in the man himself."

Berthelot had informed him of an event which was then hotly discussed—the publication by Pius IX of his Encyclical *Quanta Cura,* with its appended Syllabus, in which the author of the famous *Life* had his own portion. Renan's observations in reply, dated from Alexandretta, January 22, 1865, make so highly significant a forecast of things which have since fallen out, or which seem likely to happen, that it deserves to be quoted. He predicts a strong Gallican reaction supported by the State; but a national Church in France could never live happily, for it would be worse than the present situation. A schism was inevitable, not external, but within the Church itself. " In three or four years the Gallican party of Darboy, etc., will cease to exist." This, we may remark, came about after 1870 and the Vatican Council. Renan continues, " There will be two fractions of Catholics enraged against each other, one wild with reaction, the other entangled in a network of changes, and really Protestant. At last the State will draw itself out of these disputes, and separation will take place. But all that will bring about strange troubles (*déchirements*), which will occupy the end of this century." Renan was by no means always a true prophet; but the man who set down

these lines forty years ago had the gift of
vision.

To Antioch they went in fair weather—a difficult journey; thence by sea to Athens, where the
travellers arrived in February, 1865. This was
a culminating moment in Renan's life. He saw
now " the absolute perfection of the Greek ideals,"
and he felt dazzled by their profound, their infinite charm. He could not tear himself away
from the Acropolis; Athena became to him the
symbol of beauty, intellect, wisdom; and he poured
forth his prayer in ecstatic smiling dithyrambs to
his Greek Madonna, with a fervor that would
have touched Sophocles. The lovely Erechtheum
wins his admiration at once; but he comes only by
degrees to understand how great, how majestic, is
the Parthenon. In a vivid page he groups the
monuments, and then continues, " The spirit of all
that has been excellently rendered by Michelet.
His Athens is perfectly right. The incomparable
superiority of the Greek world, the true and simple grandeur of all it has left behind, that is what
strikes one on every side. *There* are the real
' great men,' and I am less attentive to the want
of literary talent in a certain preface "—which
Napoleon III had just then published to his fragment on Julius Cæsar—" than to the limited horizon which prevents its author from seeing beyond

the Roman world. That, by the bye, is a French peculiarity. France can never travel farther than Rome. Whatever it has attempted in the guise of Hellenic art has always been Roman."

The longer Syrian exploration had to be given up. From Athens to Smyrna is a short and not unpleasant voyage, which after six weeks in Attica Renan undertook. He went by rail to Ephesus, and then "plunged," as he said, into Asia Minor, in quest of the Apostolic Churches. It was a hazardous thing to do, but the fine-toned landscapes which adorn his *St. Paul,* especially those of the Lycian interior, rewarded him and his brave companion for their fatigues. He attempted, on his homeward journey, to reach the harbor of Patmos from Scala Nova; winds and waves did battle against him, and, after tossing about for fifty-two hours on rough waters, he was compelled to turn back.

At Smyrna we find our travellers once more, on May 6, 1865, bound for Athens a second time. They saw Mycenæ, Tiryns, Corinth; embarked for Salonica; traversed Macedonia during a favorable season; and ended at Constantinople a series of expeditions which would have done credit to Layard or Burton. What Renan said in disparagement of Stamboul, much as he admired Saint Sophia and the picturesque of sea and shore, is worth reading. Fresh from the glories of Athens, he could not bear the city which Constantine set up " to be the everlasting capital of intrigue and baseness." He would never come there again.

On this word his correspondence with Berthelot breaks off until the eve of 1870, although we possess long and interesting letters written to him by the now illustrious chemist who, in October, 1869, accompanied the Empress Eugénie, when she went to Egypt for the opening of that new waterway between East and West, the Suez Canal.

But our concern is with Renan the historian. *Les Apôtres* came out in 1866, *St. Paul* in 1869; and these form a connected narrative which has a unity of its own. To *Les Apôtres* was prefixed one of those fascinating but superficial prologues wherein the writer discoursed pleasantly of himself, his authorities, and things in general. It is a very pretty piece, sparkling with irony, gracious to the " good Luke," whose Gospel and Acts had been too much undervalued, and eloquent on the claims of religious peace, which could always be secured by giving up a little more dogma. During the stormy scenes of the French National Assembly there was an incident, tragi-comic and quite without consequence, known as " le baiser de Lamourette," which Carlyle translates as " the Delilah kiss." We are put in mind of it when M. Renan, whose deity is in the making, entreats Christians of every color to defend their interests by sacrificing all their principles.

From a spirit so curiously insensible to the real issue, we shall not look for any treatment of the Resurrection more profound than the despised eighteenth century had bequeathed to him. Renan's language is tender, nay, unctuous—we cannot escape the recurrent epithet—but he alternates, like a son of the *Aufklärung,* between theories of imposture and theories of expectant delusion. He will not accept the witness, as it has been called, of the empty tomb; he declines the force of St. Paul's spiritual experience. When he needs delusion, he summons up Mary Magdalene, " queen and patroness of idealists," by whose dream on Easter morning the world has won its vision of joy. But imposture claims its turn; " quelque petite supercherie," some trifling act of trickery, some pious fraud, must have taken place on the part of disciples unknown, who were certainly not victims of hallucination. Let us not look too narrowly into the facts, he says, any more than we did when the mighty works of Christ were in question. Only by such ambiguous means can a religion be founded; not by clean-handed philosophers, but by men and women of the people, who create the gods before which they afterward fall down in worship.

So much for the "empty tomb." What, we ask, on leaving this cloud-land of illusion, extravagance, and fever-dreams, are we to make of St. Paul, who cannot have cherished anticipations about Jesus, for he never set eyes on Him in the flesh, and who breathed out threatenings and slaughter against His followers? Can St. Paul be explained away under a psychological rubric borrowed from physicians?

Renan does not like to be cross-examined in so rude a fashion. By judicious mingling of times and seasons, by reading back into the Pharisee that which the Apostle has told us of his later ecstasies, by supposing him to have been a neurotic subject from his youth up, and by comparing this sudden change, effected without visible antecedents, to Lamennais' apostasy, which took years to accomplish, the story-teller gets rid of a miracle that in its circumstances was no less beyond what we have learned about the laws of Nature than was the Resurrection itself. Any incident, he assures us, will suffice when we can take refuge in psychology—a thunder-storm, the noonday heat, the coming on of a fever such as Renan had himself experienced at Amschit. That nothing of the kind is mentioned by St. Paul or in the Acts can make no difference. Revelation not being admissible, hallucination is the only key to a portent of which the witness may not be set down as a deliberate impostor.

Yet, as is well known, Ferdinand Christian Baur could never feel satisfied that this was the true account of Saul's conversion. The Apostle, who told his own story again and again, had but one explanation, from which he did not draw back in any presence. But to allow it, Renan must have accepted the existence of a spiritual unseen world encompassing the world in which we live and move. That was impossible. He could never grant that an intellect superior to the human was extant in the universe, or that death of the body did not involve extinction of the spirit. His great first principle, which admitted only of "phenomena," and was identical with Comte's, carried with it these consequences. To a deeper science they appear singularly inadequate, and even incredible, as they are surely destructive of all that mankind has cherished under the name of religion.

These defects, which forever divide Renan from the company of spiritual seers in whose light humanity lives, must not blind us to his merits as an artist, a scholar, and an historian. The insatiable curiosity of a spirit untamed was learning to concentrate its powers on one subject, enough for a lifetime, the transformation of the Roman Empire into the Holy Catholic Church. During eighteen years Renan was intent on this great epic, which he viewed in all its stages and at every centre where it had left a record. In dedicating *St. Paul* to his wife, Cornélie, he says, "We have seen together Ephesus and Antioch, Philippi and Thessalonica, Athens and Corinth, Colossæ and Laodicæa. . . . At Seleucia, standing on the disjointed stones of its ancient mole, we felt a little envious of the Apostles, who there set sail to conquer the world, full of a burning faith in the Kingdom of God."

He was already familiar with Rome, to which those hopes and fears had all converged. He lived day by day among the reminiscences of antiquity. His own large reading, the consultation of experts in Eastern lore, and the insight which his Catholic bringing up had given him into the circumstances that call forth new religious associations, fitted him admirably for some part of his task. Unlike Gibbon, he is reverent in dealing with Saints and Martyrs; but he cannot, like Gibbon, draw a strong and lively picture in a few firm strokes. His descriptions are picturesque; his personages, on the other hand, leave us uncertain whether we should know them if they suddenly came before us. In grasping the moral and social causes to which Christianity owed its triumph, he is far more successful. Yet, even here, when he traces the decline of Paganism, especially among the Greeks, he might have borrowed with advantage from Plutarch and Pausanias details, both light and sombre, which would have added to the somewhat low relief of too abstract a style.

Always by preference classic, and even, one may say, Catholic, as opposed to the Protestant of a fierce controversial type, Renan, who looked upon St. Paul as the father of Luther and Calvin, as a Hebrew in his very revolt from what was afterward the Talmud, and as a theologian who justified the whole scheme of sin and redemption, could not forbear to exhibit the great Apostle in a crude light.

St. Paul's outward and inward man are to this worshipper of Apollo equally displeasing, and on the same ground, their lack of beautiful form. Trusting to late works, for instance, the *Philopatris,* the writer indulges himself in a caricature which might very well describe Thersites, but is surely not worthy of a place in history. We know better how to judge of a style which is not apocryphal like this fancied portrait, but which lies open to our view in St. Paul's Epistles. It is, we grant, neither Attic nor Ionic; yet it is endowed with energy so astonishing that for eighteen hundred years it has borne to be read in all the churches without losing any of its power.

Renan, who detested writing letters, allowed to

St. Paul this inferior kind of composition; it
" suited his feverish activity, his need of express-
ing in a moment what he felt." And the critic
sums him up, " Lively, rude, polished, mischievous, sarcastic, then all at once tender, delicate,
almost pretty and coaxing, with phrases happy and
subtle in a high degree, toning down his manner
with reticences, reservations, infinite safeguards,
sly allusions, cloaked ironies, he could not but
excel in a manner which is, before all things, spontaneous. The epistolary turn of St. Paul is the
most individual that ever was. His language, so
to speak, is brayed in a mortar; no two sentences
follow in succession. It would be impossible for
anyone to set aside more boldly the logic, I do not
say of Greek, but of human speech altogether.
We might call it a rapid conversation taken down
in shorthand, then repeated without corrections."

But in spite of his marvellously ardent spirit, the
Apostle has no great store of phrases. " A single
word haunts him "; he will come back to it in
season and out of season for a whole page; " not
that his mind is barren, it is only troubled; he
never thinks a second time about style." Hence,
concludes Renan, his Epistles, though strikingly
original, have no charm. Nevertheless, a judge
as competent as the French critic, we mean Cardinal Newman, dwells on St. Paul's " gift of sym-

pathy," and goes so far as to call him, " this sweetest of inspired writers, this most touching and winning of teachers."   Such, too, was the opinion of St. John Chrysostom, who, as a Syrian and a Greek orator, was peculiarly intimate with the Pauline temperament.

Not, then, a great artist, according to Renan, the Apostle is likewise not a learned Hellene; nor a mystic, although rapt to the third Heaven; nor is he eminently a saint.   He stands far behind the " friends of Jesus," who founded the Christian tradition and wrote the Gospels.   He is the man of action, the conquering missionary, " fierce, harsh, difficult," abounding in dogmas and formulas, not in gracious parables like the divine Master; his very faith is a struggle.   But he had the genius to discern that, if ever men embraced a universal religion, it would not be one in which the rites and ceremonies of Judaism were made obligatory on all nations.   How different from Mohammed, whose disciples cannot live outside certain degrees of latitude, and whose teaching everywhere betrays the influence of Arab customs and the desert!   St. Paul, in this view, is the second founder of Christianity; when he pursues the track of Jewish propaganda from synagogue to synagogue along the shores of the Mediterranean, he is fulfilling the ancient prophecies that made of Israel an apostle to the Gentiles. He did more than write the first chapter of dogmatic theology in his Roman Letter; he taught the West how it might be Christian, yet escape from the yoke of a foreign law; and by so doing he substituted Rome for Jerusalem, the Vatican for Mount Zion, as " the mountain of the Lord, the house of the God of Jacob."

To travel with St. Paul on his missionary voyages has been a favorite occupation in modern books. We cannot undertake, as Renan did, to visit those ruined cities: Antioch, with its amphitheatre of hills; the valley of the Lycus or the Mæander; Ephesus, the shrine of Artemis; Alexandria Troas, or Philippi, standing out boldly in its fruitful plain. Paul before the Areopagus offers to our view a contrast to which only Paul in the presence of Nero may suggest a parallel. These are two moments in history when the drama of a world's fate is shown openly on the stage. But Renan is not to be captivated by that exquisite pleading in the seventeenth of Acts on behalf of the " unknown God," whose revelation was at hand. All he can perceive is a " small ugly Jew " decreeing that the marble gods and their temples shall pass away; an " iconoclast " whose eyes are shut to the beauty which he condemns, and who takes Athena for an idol.

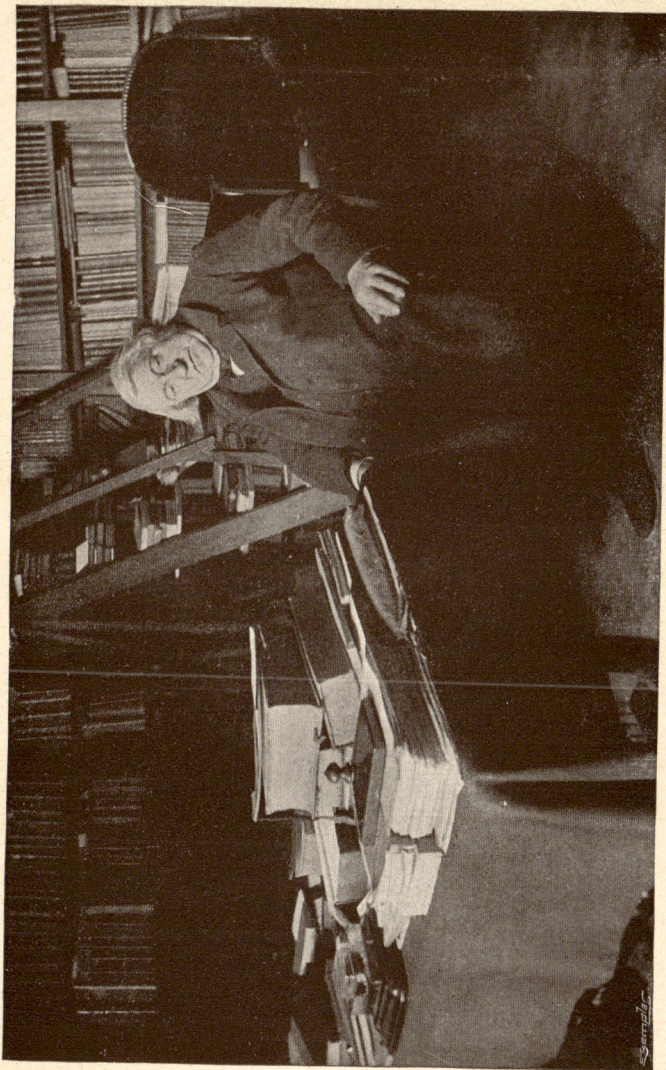

Ernest Renan in his Study.
Photo Dornac

The artist in Renan cries out with tears against
that sacrilege. Yet he was aware, for he had read
Aristophanes, that no degree of culture, however
finely expressed, no statues or poems, though supremely fair, could save the Athenians from unspeakable degradation. St. Paul knew it better
than he, not by studying antique remains on the
spot or in dead museums, but by an experience
which daily and hourly came before his eyes in
every city of that corrupt world. Culture, says
our critic, was unable to believe in the Resurrection. Nevertheless, he observes, in the discourse
of St. Paul on the Hill of Mars, we are witnessing
a first attempt to reconcile the supernatural with
science, to translate Christian and Jewish thought
into Greek; Clement of Alexandria and Origen
were to follow the example by and by. But the
reconciliation would never find its opportunity in
Athens.

The school of Tübingen had always attracted
Renan by its dissolving criticism; it repelled him,
for he was French and moderate in temper, by
what he considered its extravagance. From it he
borrowed lavishly in treating of the dissensions
which broke out between St. Paul and his Jewish
brethren, as recorded in the Acts and the Epistles,
but he declined to go the whole way. He, too,
made much of the pseudo-Clementine literature,

which is Ebionite, Petrine, and zealous for the
rights of Jerusalem. He was willing to identify
St. Paul with Simon Magus, whom, in those po-
lemical fictions, St. Peter follows everywhere and
denounces as the "enemy" or the Antichrist. On
the other hand, in St. Luke he recognized a disciple
and apologist of St. Paul; and he was reluctant
to deny the historical value of that passage in itself
so remarkable, which brings together St. Peter and
the Roman Cornelius, and thus affords a meeting
ground for the tolerant practices of both Apostles.

In like manner he would now be termed conservative as regards the Pauline writings, which
he divides into three classes, rejecting only those
to Timothy and Titus, while assigning to some
unknown hand the Epistle to the Hebrews, perhaps to Barnabas. He addressed a warning in
sharp language to the pedants who have determined *a priori* how the Apostle must have written.
And he added, not unfairly, that German professors, wrangling among themselves in lecture and
dissertation, were the last who would be likely to
understand how a popular religion had begun. In
his view, therefore, no such complete antagonism
existed, even between St. Paul and the party of
legal zealots represented by St. James, as would
hinder them from sharing in the common effort
to spread their faith. He was thus not very far

off, when we consider his principles, from the orthodox position which has combined in the same
New Testament Paul and James and John, the
Apocalypse and the Epistle to the Romans, as
chapters which make up severally the one Divine
message.

But nothing would induce him to like St. Paul.
" After having been for three hundred years,
thanks to Protestantism, the Christian doctor *par
excellence,* Paul is now coming to an end of his
reign." So the volume concludes; and Matthew
Arnold's comment may follow: " All through his
book M. Renan is possessed with a sense of this
close relationship between St. Paul and Protestantism. Protestantism has made Paul, he says; Pauline doctrine is identified with Protestant doctrine;
Paul is a Protestant doctor, and the counterpart of
Luther. M. Renan has a strong distaste for
Protestantism, and this distaste extends itself to
the Protestant Paul. The reign of this Protestant
is now coming to an end, and such a consummation
evidently has M. Renan's approval."

It had undoubtedly. Much as the freethinking
Herder at one time drew the student's admiration
(who knew little about him except his free-
thought) toward real Protestants, orthodox or
liberal, he felt something like aversion. " I am
often asked by German Christians," he said in a

phrase which was clamorously taken up, " what do I make of sin? *Mon Dieu,* I believe that I suppress it." A brilliant epigram; but even in his liveliest days Renan had seen the writing on the wall which told France that its sin would find it out. In the preface to *St. Paul* these words stand on record, " Our youthful age saw melancholy times; and I dread lest Fate should show us no good before we die. Some enormous mistakes are driving our country into the abyss; when we point them out we are met with smiles." His *Questions Contemporaines,* published in 1868, holds the warning, strongly and almost passionately uttered, to which these forebodings allude. It was an indictment of the French Revolution, no less emphatic than Edmund Burke's, and so much better warranted that a succession of calamities had set on it their seal.

One passage became immediately the war-cry of all those who still clung to the alliance between throne and altar. It spoke of the Revolution as an experiment which had failed. Only a single kind of inequality was left, that of fortune, in a State which took to itself all things else; which created an intellectual desert for the sake of Paris; which degraded social service into mere administration; which put an end to the growth of colonies; and which could not be sure of the future.

Bankruptcy was inevitable with a code of laws
" that seemed to have been made for a citizen committed to the foundling hospital at birth and dying
a bachelor "; laws that made every collective and
enduring work impossible; that divided the father
from his children, the husband from his wife; and
that, instead of giving property a moral value,
turned it into the symbol of sensuous enjoyment.
What could such laws bring forth but a world of
pygmies and rebels?

On the other hand, said Renan, look at Prussia.
There philosophy, government, character were
joined in a public task; a great Germany, wise and
liberal, was coming to the birth. Let France not
attempt a military organization like the Prussian,
unless it was prepared to adopt the moral training
on which that system was founded. German science, German universities, the German method of
handling religion, these were prerequisites to a
German army. For such a people victory would
be assured. But " in the fatal round of revolutions, deep calleth unto deep. Examples may be
cited of nations which, having gone down into that
hell of Dante, have come out again alive. What
shall we say of the nation that has escaped from
it and yet will plunge into it once more, nay, even
twice and thrice? "

CHAPTER VI

PARIS AND JERUSALEM

DESTINY, which is Providence judging the world, was not long in giving the answer. A Liberal Opposition had taken to driving the chariot of the sun, while Phœbus-Napoleon slept. " Dormirà sempre," said Renan, who in May, 1869, for one short instant, fancied that he had a call to political action. He put out his manifesto in big letters on the walls of many villages, addressing the district of Meaux in philosophic terms. " No revolution! " he cried. " No war! A war would be as great a disaster as revolution." He was for peace, retrenchment and reform. But Cassandra did not get elected. The clerical influence on one side, the Jacobin on another, were dead against a man whose party, if it could be said anywhere to exist, had no command over the multitude. As on a previous occasion, he found solace for his defeat in travelling. Prince Napoleon took him in the summer of 1870 on an expedition to the Arctic Circle. He paid a flying visit to Inverness and coasted along the fiords of Norway. There was talk of sailing to Spitzbergen. From Storen near Trondheim, on July 11, Renan despatched a gay letter to Berthelot, full of these plans and projects. At Tromsöe, one week later, a telegram informed the Prince that war with Prussia was certain and immediate.

"A fit of madness, an absolute crime," exclaimed Renan when the news was brought. But the crime had been committed, and the travellers hastened back to France. In his pleasant summer home at Sèvres the disconcerted idealist, who had been proposing a reduction of the French army, looked on while his philosophers from beyond the Rhine proved what science could do with a rifle on its shoulder. His unhappy countrymen were not only suffering reverses on a hundred battle-fields; they were victims of the "decomposition of society" against which he had raised his voice. Did he and his *Life of Jesus* count for nothing in that irretrievable disaster, as a symptom, if not as a cause? Years afterward, in the *Priest of Nemi,* one Ganeo lays down the philosophy of cowardice, which sees in flight the chance of enjoyment to-morrow. The French soldiers fought, indeed, with proverbial courage; but they had lost religion for the greater part; they were wanting in stamina, physical and mental; their generals were victims or patrons of intrigue; the ice of the Beresina broke under them, and the flood carried them away.

For Renan the " downfall " was more than a public misfortune, however anticipated; it came as a private grief to him. His whole character underwent a change in the " Terrible Year." Edmond de Goncourt, who had made his acquaintance at the literary dinners in the Café Brébant, gives us a description of the man, dated May 25, 1868, before these things came to pass. " Called on Renan," he writes, " the fourth storey in Rue Vanneau—a small set of rooms, *bourgeois* and neat, the furniture in green plush, heads by Ary Scheffer on the walls, and among keepsakes from Dunkirk the hand of a woman delicately moulded. Through an open door the library is visible, shelves in white wood, large unbound volumes lying in stacks on the floor, the tools of learning, mediæval or Eastern, quartos of all kinds, a section of a Japanese dictionary, and on a small table the slumbering proofs of *St. Paul.* Out of the two windows an immense prospect, one of those forests of verdure hidden among the walls and stones of Paris; it is the Parc Galliera, the ocean of treetops over which appear sacred buildings, domes, bell-towers, something of the pious horizon of Rome. The man himself seems always more charming and affectionately polite. He is the pattern of moral gracefulness in a body far from graceful; the apostle of doubt has the high intellectual good-nature of a priest of science."

This appreciation does not go deeper than the surface; but all the accounts we find of Renan bear it out. In a universal shipwreck, however, to be amiable is no great help; the apostle of doubt was torn by emotions which set in fierce antagonism his devotion to science and his love for France. Nor can the latter be doubted, although it bore little resemblance to Gambetta's fury and was rather old-Breton than new-democratic in its coloring. He would have rejoiced at a conquest of Paris by Herder and Goethe; in Bismarck and the Red Prince he could discern simply the Barbarians. He was unjust—pardonably in so sudden and frightful a storm of war; but those who have lingered among the ruins of the Castle at Heidelberg, and who remember what Louis XIV made of the Palatinate, will be thankful that no French soldiers crossed the Rhine in 1870. Renan tells us, without a blush, that if he had been ever compelled to enlist he should have deserted. When he saw the troops marching out in August, 1870, along the Boulevards he despised them. "Not a man there," he said, "is capable of a virtuous act." He was for peace at almost any price. In September, 1870, his letter to David Strauss pleaded, however, against the violent seizure of Alsace and Lorraine, without regard to the will of the inhabitants. Not race, but history, made a nation. He reminded his German friends that Russia was the coming danger. Strauss translated this eloquent epistle, bound it up with his own reply, and sold it for the benefit of the German wounded. Renan could not help expending a little irony on this performance when it came to his ears. " Heaven forbid," he said smiling, " that I should quarrel with you over a point of copyright. The work for which you lay me under contribution is a work of humanity; and if my humble prose has purchased a few cigars for the men that plundered my cottage at Sèvres, I thank you for the opportunity you have given me of obeying some precepts of Jesus which I believe to be quite genuine. But remark certain slight differences. Had you permitted me to publish one of your writings, never, oh never, should I have thought of selling it on behalf of our Hôtel des Invalides. Your aim misleads you; passion will not suffer you to heed those fancies of a worn-out people which are known as tact and good taste."

Unhappy France! Betrayed, as Renan was never weary of saying, in February, 1848, when Louis Philippe capitulated to a mob in the streets; bound and gagged by the midnight crime of December, 1851; it had been brought to a pass where, he continued bitterly, "the good God vanished, to make room for an inflexible *Sebaoth,* who could only be touched by the moral delicacy of Uhlans, the undoubted excellence of Prussian bombshells." The horrible reign of violence had set in. Napoleon III was swept into the gutter. And Kant's disciples laid siege to Paris with a stern categorical imperative, which blazed out in sheets of flame on the wintry sky and rained upon Neuilly a tempest of fire.

What could the peaceful professor do in this tumult? Like the two millions of Paris he had no retreat. He stayed in his old house, lived on his dole of black bread and salt meat, attended the dinner at Magny's where a small company foregathered still, and listened while Berthelot, who was the chemist of the Third Republic, denounced Trochu and wrung his hands over the infinite disorder that reigned in high places. Strange food was eaten by the besieged philosophers and men of letters. Goncourt relates, with a grim countenance, how they were compelled, at last, to eat dog, disguised as mutton, and how Renan rushed with loathing from the banquet. A singular conclusion to his German studies! But he would not indulge, as even better men did, in the hope of revenge. In November, when Metz had fallen and Gambetta was urging forward those untrained levies which did but prolong the agony of France, Renan braved public opinion by advising that a Parliament should be called and peace made. He could not win a hearing, but he had done his duty.

A conversation at Brébant's, taken down without leave by Goncourt, on September 6, 1870, became in after times celebrated. The guests were calling out for vengeance on the invader, who would soon be persuading them to devour unclean meats and broth of abominable things, when Renan protested. The Germans were a superior race —great in war as in science generally; and as for revenge, " Perish France," he cried, rising to his feet, " perish our country; above it all is the kingdom of Duty and Reason." He was met with shouts of execration. " No," thundered St. Victor, " we are not going to be esthetes and Byzantines; there is nothing above our country." Renan, says the narrator, had quitted his place and was moving round the table with uncertain steps, waving his short arms in the air, and reciting verses from the Bible. " All is there," he reiterated, adding as he went to the window, from which the evening promenade of Parisians was visible, " Look, what will save us is the effeminacy of that population."

The hero of this remarkable scene denied it in
1890 almost with petulance, but it shows the man,
and was not invented.   His *Intellectual and Moral
Reform,* composed during the siege, tells a like
story in words more carefully chosen.   " The country of idealists," he repeated, in spite of contradiction, " is wherever they may think freely."   The
Prussian bombardment drove him, in January,
1871, from his house on the left bank of the Seine;
but it could not alter principles which were the
fruit of a life's meditation.   Every day his wrath
against government by popular suffrage grew more
fierce.   " Civilization has always been a creation
of aristocracy, upheld by a small number," he told
Berthelot in an historic letter.   He preferred the
House of Orleans to any Republic.   It was the
ignorant peasantry that had raised Louis Napoleon to his dictatorship.   This Third Republic
would never have existed but for " presumptuous
imbeciles "—he meant especially Gambetta—rhet-
oricians from the south who, as in 1789, had
proved too much for the national good sense with
their frothy eloquence.

On the other hand, St. Cloud was a heap of
smoking ashes; Auteuil lay bare beneath such a
hailstorm of shells as made of it one ruin; on
January 18, 1871, King William was crowned
German Emperor at Versailles amid " all the

glories of France." Rumors flew about that Paris itself would be burned, if it did not surrender. "We shall witness a fresh Apocalypse," said Renan, sighing deeply.

The capitulation arrived; he saw his Germans march down through the Champs Elysées to the Place de la Concorde, as in a city of the dead. Then he went back home; but a month had scarcely elapsed when the National Guard, a pretorian democracy, proclaimed the Commune; and while he was quoting Scripture and Spinoza, "To arms!" resounded once more along the Boulevards. "The weakness, the hesitation, of Government has ruined us," said this enlightened critic, whose judgment of M. Thiers, when he abandoned the Capital, has been confirmed by history. Could France live again? Had corruption seized its vital parts? He asked the question, but hardly dared to answer it.

His intention had been to remain in Paris, provided there were not a second investment by the Prussians. But he could not expose his family to a growing risk; about April 28, after a month of the Commune, he fled with them to the dismantled cottage at Sèvres which now gave refuge to sixteen persons. Berthelot, who was at Honfleur, had been invited to England; but Renan dissuaded him from going in forcible language,

though he almost expected to see France broken
up and the nation perish. He felt more than ever.
that in dethroning her Royal House she had committed the unpardonable sin, the crime against history. Liberals—he named Littré and Henri Mar-
tin—dealt with human affairs in too simple a
manner. Their aim was right, their system
childish.

The ink of these reflections was hardly dry when
a cloudburst of shells from the advancing army
fell on Sèvres and obliged Renan to decamp. He
passed on with his household to Versailles. The
last day of the Commune, Sunday, May 28, 1871,
dawned in blood and fire. He was then writing
from Sèvres in his old house, and toward nightfall
he watched the great sulphurous conflagration
which lit up with a yellow glare the sky toward
the east. There he might view the end of a " crim-
inal extravagance," the reduction to the absurd
of theories that took not into account elements and
forces which were no less real than indispensable
to civilized life. Equality, it seemed to him, never
had existed among nations or individuals. " The
true foundation of kindness," he wrote in those
fearful days, " is to believe in a providential order,
where each thing has its place and its rank, its use
and its necessity." But he saw religion dying
round him, and he said, " We are living on

the shadow of a shade. By what will men live after us?"

Though fearing that the soul of France had been mortally wounded in 1789 and 1793, Renan proposed in his *Reform Intellectual and Moral* a plan which no one would ever have deduced from the tastes of so resolutely classical a scholar. In literature he was becoming more and more the Greek who was condemned to write in French, and who made the best of it. But his politics were German, feudal, and aristocratic.

To explain his position in few words is not easy. Englishmen have seldom perceived how close is the connection between the Imperial Roman Law and the Code Napoléon; neither do they seem to realize that democracy in Latin countries is altogether unlike what we call by the name in these islands or in the United States. For on the Continent it has drawn from Justinian's *Pandects* the twofold element of an equality without distinctions and a despotism without any court of appeal. Now the French Revolution was nothing but this Roman Law dressed in modern costume, applied to an order of things which had grown out of quite different principles, and which, therefore, it could only pull down. Renan had a clear view of the opposition between these two forms, the Imperial and the Feudal. He held that State

Socialism could not fail to be the outcome of French democracy; that private property must be defended on a far different system; and that without the principle of hereditary succession, made permanent in a royal line, civilized Europe would be at the mercy of adventurers—of soldiers like Bonaparte, or lawyers like Gambetta. The Gauls had triumphed over the Franks when Louis XVI was executed, but they could only break with so resplendent a past by falling into the pit of an ignoble anarchy. The omnipotent State would never heal these woes, for it was their very source and their aggravation.

Freedom, he went on to argue, was not, as people fancied, a mere means; it was an end in itself, a permanent condition of progress; and the Barbarians that overthrew the Western Empire had established freedom. For what is freedom if not the independence of individuals, and the right of private associations to manage their own affairs? But these are precisely the things which no government issuing from the Revolution will endure. Yet progress does not come from without; virtue cannot be decreed by Act of Parliament. France had "sown her gardens of Adonis, and hoped that the sun would fertilize flowers which had no root"; her idea of freedom was a tyranny pressing on all alike, and she had robbed her citizens of the courage to think and to will. The true social life was a part of the divine life itself, and its last word was conscience.

To call this indictment of the Revolution un-patriotic was much easier than to answer it. Per-haps a candid opponent, while allowing its chief articles, would reply that not one or two, but all the old Sibylline books had been burned, and that democracy on the Roman system was in possession, while the better form of which Renan dreamed could simply not be created so late in the day. This, at all events, is true; that with piercing in-sight he who was, in other respects, much of a dilettante, had seen what scarcely a Liberal in any land had taken to heart, the value of an historical past to a nation, and the penalty exacted for dis-regard of it. Whether the Latin peoples were ever to enjoy an ordered freedom, in Church or State, might be a problem. But rare, surely, was the merit of an observer who had never lived among free men, yet who drew so distinctly the line which divides Europe into rival camps, and which alone will account for the political vicissi-tudes of the nineteenth century, though it has been overlooked on all sides.

No one, however, was inclined to follow Re-nan's lead. The old factions tore their country asunder; Henry V waved his white flag; the Bonapartes and the House of Orleans struck their traditional attitudes; the Republic, slowly gathering might, threw off and exiled the families which had reigned in France. Under this Government of the baser sort Renan was destined to live out his days. He counted for nothing in the world of politics. The Chair of Hebrew had been restored to him in 1870. When the Commune had bled its last, bayonetted and shot to death by MacMahon, the professor, now an important man in his College, went to Italy, that he might renew his acquaintance with Rome, and evoke from the ruins of the Forum and the Palatine the ghost of Nero.

He was caught once more by the ancient charm; his imagination kindled, and under that impulse he produced his *Antichrist,* a work of art, perhaps the most brilliant of all that he has left us. It amused and delighted him. " I will not deny," he said by way of introduction to it, " that a taste for history, the incomparable pleasure which one has in seeing unrolled before one the spectacle of mankind, has drawn me on in this volume. Sometimes I have rebuked myself for enjoying life so keenly in my workshop, while my poor country was consumed in a slow agony; but my conscience is at rest." He had done what in him lay to prevent or to heal the troubles of the time. He could not act the charlatan. This very book, though addressed to the curious and the artistic, not to the crowd, had its own moral, " triumphant vice denounced when at its height in sublime accents by the saints." " More than ever am I convinced," said the writer, " that religion is not a self-inflicted deception; that it answers to an object outside of us; and that he who obeys its inspiration is well guided." What such a confession amounted to we shall learn by and by from the *Philosophic Dialogues,* thrown down on paper at Versailles in 1871, but not given to the world until years had passed.

His present subject was Nero, the true Antichrist of the Book of Revelation. " Over against Jesus, the ideal of goodness," he warns us, " rises up a monstrous being who is the embodiment of evil. Reserved like Enoch and Elias to play his part in the world's last act, Nero completes the Christian mythology, inspires the first sacred book of the new canon, by a hideous massacre founds the primacy of the Roman Church, and sets on foot the revolution which is to make of Rome the Holy City, the second Jerusalem. At the same hour, by one of those mysterious coincidences which are not unknown in the great crises of mankind, Jerusalem is destroyed, the Temple passes away; Christianity, more and more emancipated, is free henceforth from a vanquished Judaism, and works out its own destiny."

But again the figure of St. Paul rises before us, a prisoner in Rome, as the Acts describe him, yet not hindered in preaching the gospel. Renan could by no effort overcome his repugnance to the great dogmatic teacher. St. Paul's exaltation of Jesus in the later and genuine Epistles—to the Philippians, Colossians and Ephesians—went on increasing, says his critic, until there was little to choose between his doctrine and that of the Fourth Evangelist. It was, in fact, the spirit of St. Paul, he continues, which ruled those Church assemblies from Nicæa to Chalcedon, where the creed of Christendom was definitely shaped. Renan calls him a sectary enamored of the absurd-like Tertullian, an enemy to culture, which his disciples have always flouted and thrown back. He is the father of Puritans, and by his hatred of the world, *odium generis humani*—the charge brought against Christians in Tacitus—will always provoke a reaction to those Greek ideas which he has decried in his most violent pages. The Letters to Titus and Timothy are not of St. Paul's composition, according to Renan, but, as in an historical romance, they picture not untruly his mind, as well as his anticipations, when the catastrophe which ended him was approaching.

St. Paul had felt that he must bear witness to his Master in Rome, and a vision of Jesus confirmed the resolve he had taken. That appeal to Cæsar and his eventful voyage determined St. Peter to follow him. The two Apostles were friends, although Peter could not boldly take sides with Paul against James and John, champions of legal or Ebionite principles. But by quoting, as he does, from the Pauline writings in his one authentic missive, dated at the Roman Babylon, the Prince of the Apostles refutes that conception of Baur which makes no allowance for Jewish freedom of speech, and which is too absolute to be trustworthy.

Yet St. Peter it was, continues Renan, who gave the Roman Church its supreme place in Christendom. The poor Syrian emigrant who found a home in the Ghetto beyond Tiber, at the foot of the Janiculum, began in effect that wonderful dynasty which succeeded to all the splendor and more than the prerogatives of the Cæsars. St. John also, the son of thunder to whom we owe the Apocalypse, by his opposition of Rome to Jerusalem, admits or recognizes the part that was to be enacted by the Imperial City in God's counsels. The seer had accompanied St. Peter, perhaps had undergone a trial when the Neronian persecution broke out. Last of all, the so-called Epistle to the Hebrews was dictated by the same events, probably sent from Ephesus to the Roman Christians, and abounds in Pauline ideas. Thus, if we glance back over the progress of the new religion, we see it advancing from Jerusalem to Antioch, from Antioch to Ephesus, from Ephesus to Rome. And at Rome the chief Apostles meet in their several ways to suffer martyrdom, while Luke, the follower of St. Paul, and John Mark, the disciple of St. Peter, prepare in the world's Capital to write their biography of Jesus.

To this unexampled situation, in which elements at once diverse and strong were to be fused together, Nero supplies the centre, the crisis, and the issue. Waiving aside the dreams of mystics, Renan, with supreme good sense, fixes on history as a clew to the Apocalypse. He accepts, indeed, too lightly the grotesque supposition that St. Paul everywhere lies concealed beneath opprobrious names and types in that " written ecstasy "—to use the admirable definition which Balzac once gave of it. But on such a point we need not stop to argue. That Nero is the subject of St. John's anathemas, and that under the veil of strange words, cabalistic numbers and heaped-up symbols, the revolutions of the Roman Empire have been shadowed forth, is a theory which explains what would otherwise be incomprehensible. Nor was that theory unknown to the generation immediately following the Apostolic age. How it fell into discredit, while the Book of Revelation itself was doubted or left among the Apocrypha by the Eastern Fathers, Renan has described in a suggestive chapter. These questions are for theologians. The reading public, which is incompetent to decide them, will be more taken with his sketch of Roman life and manners when Nero, the crazy artist, was king.

That "unfortunate young man" must have appeared to the Renan who utters his paradoxes in Goncourt's *Journal* as a singularly modern type. He is decadent, Parisian, nay, in the slang of the artist, *un raté,* one who has attempted great things and achieved none of them. He cannot be presented in self-respecting language as he really was. The French biographer has left unquoted his Roman authors—laudably enough, for they defy translation in our Christian speech—at the most melancholy turns of the story. Such reticence has a grave disadvantage; we may be led to think of the monster almost with indulgence, forgetting his crimes to smile at his extravagances.

However, it is certainly true that " madness was in the air "; and that " if we except the groups of aristocratic Romans who were destined to arrive at power with Nerva and Trajan, a general want

of seriousness tempted men the most considerable
in some sort to play with life." The arbiter of
elegance was Petronius; the preacher, himself not
deeply in earnest, was Seneca, from whom our
dilettante borrows a significant phrase, applicable
to the Paris of his own day, " Intemperantia lit-
teratum laboramus," we are suffering from a
plague of literature. But no one wrote or painted
or sculptured beautiful things any more. Nero
himself is defined as a literary perversion, whose
greatest achievement was setting fire to old Rome.

This burning up of ancient palaces and sacred
shrines marks the birthday of another Rome,
Christian, nay Catholic, which rose amid flames
and slaughter in the Vatican Circus of Nero, where
St. Peter's Confession now stands. Early writings
connect the persecution so vividly described by
Tacitus with the martyrdom of both Apostles.
Renan sees no ground for doubting the statement;
but he adds a conjecture that in some way the
Jewish enemies of a rapidly growing faith were
instigated by jealousy to denounce their former
brethren. At all events " after the day when Jesus
expired on Golgotha, that day of festival in Nero's
gardens (we may fix it about August 1, in the
year 64 A.D.) was the most solemn in Christian
history."

From Parisian decadents Renan had learned

how to represent, "intus et in cute," the elegant
parricide, actor, singer and chariot-driver who
gave to Rome its baptism of blood. He lingered
even a little too complacently over the art which
from flowers of evil distils a deadly bouquet. He
was not altogether so serious as his dreadful subject demanded. But his second chapter, dealing
with revolted Judæa, the siege of Jerusalem, and
Nero's downfall, required to be written in another
key, of which the note was struck by his experi-
ences during the Commune. Had the Temple
continued to exist, with its law and its sacrifices,
how could St. Paul's free spiritual religion have
survived? The Fourth Gospel is not to be distinguished on this point from the Epistle to the
Romans; in both it is the assertion of Jesus and
His true disciples that " not in this mountain nor
yet at Jerusalem shall ye worship the Father."
An infatuation which amazed the Roman world,
a frenzy breaking out in revolt, murder, and the
suicide of a whole people, brought Vespasian to
the walls of the " beloved city," as it is termed
in the Apocalypse. Then East and West fell into
confusion. Three Emperors, Galba, Otho, Vitel-
lius, passed like phantoms over the scene. Nero
became a fugitive, who heard in pursuit of him
the Furies that hunted Orestes. He disappeared;
but was he dead? Would he not come again, from

the Parthians or from Egypt, conquering and to
conquer? At this fateful moment, in the first days
of the year 69 A.D., so Renan argues, the Book of
Revelation appeared, written by St. John or at his
suggestion. It is the seal set on Old Hebrew
prophecy, the parting embrace between Gospel and
Talmud, ere they bid each other an everlasting
farewell.

How bold a thing it was to comment before all
Paris on such a work as the Apocalypse, and how
rare the skill with which the commentator fulfilled
his task, will be evident to those who have gone
through Renan's large volume, where every page
is ancient history in a modern setting. We may
liken the renegade of St. Sulpice, now a somewhat
worldly minded man, or, as a witty friend called
him, " the dandy of exegesis," compelled to look
on while Paris was burning, to Josephus, equally
a deserter, yet always a Jew, and the historian
of his nation's ruin. Josephus wrote his chronicle
for the Flavian Emperors, perhaps under their
roof on the Palatine. Renan hoped against hope
that Paris would take warning from Jerusalem.

As ever, his heart was divided. Imperial Rome
conquered by virtue of its good sense, its law which
did not involve a theocracy, its common rights of
citizenship. The Jew, the zealot, the Christian,
the monk, all akin and one as intolerant as the

other, have been, he says, a menace to civilization.
Yet the victory of Titus could not be final. Our
Western races are the flower of men, but in religion they create nothing durable or profound.
What could be expected from the prosaic Roman
ritual, the superstitions of Gaul, or even the Greek
mysteries, in comparison with ideals like the Synagogue and the Church? The heavenly Jerusalem
did, therefore, overcome Babylon when the earthly
had sunk down in flames; and the arch of Titus
records a triumph which is seen to be undone upon
the arch of Constantine.

But, says the preacher, let France read her future in that past. Every nation which devotes
itself to social and political agitation is doomed.
If it seeks a " kingdom of God," lives on general
ideas, pursues a quest of world-wide importance,
it will never be a great Power. " We are not
mistaken when we cry out to France, ' Give up
the Revolution or perish,' but yet if a single one
of its dreams should be fulfilled, the misery of
1870 and 1871 will have had its revenge." Is
this an apology for the Commune? Renan ab-
horred its excesses; but he was ever unwilling to
shut the gates of the future in the face of unknown possibilities. In daily life a peaceable and
smiling *bourgeois,* the instant he takes up his pen
he becomes a Utopian. The hero as thinker must

not be scared by the police; no transformation, in the long run, is incredible. Jerusalem fallen, the old order vanished, the Christian set free from a yoke which even St. Paul could not have unfastened, a problem of reconciliation between the new faith and the ancient Empire could not fail to arise. How it was resolved is the question which occupied three volumes and another nine years of this indefatigable career. The *Antichrist* came out in 1873, *Marcus Aurelius,* which completes the *Origins of Christianity,* was published in 1882. A full twenty-five years had been consumed in journeys, reading and composition, since the author took up his large enterprise. Only ten years remained to him; these he spent on minor works and the *History of Israel.*

A change in tone and treatment had, meanwhile, come over his writings. He had always denied miracles; but when he began the *Life of Jesus,* there was in his mind a tendency to recognize what we may term the Divine drama, something not unlike Providence, under whose guidance Greek, Hebrew, and Roman were united in a common though unconscious building up of Humanity. The doctrine of final causes, not quite in its popular sense, was admitted, was dwelt upon. Then came the catastrophe of France, and farewell to Renan's calm serenity, which had led him to believe in progress, and at one time actually to maintain that " the world made better by science will be the kingdom of the spirit, the reign of the children of God." But now he perceived that science might yield a Prussian army as its outcome, or a revolution ending in the torches of the *pétroleuses*. Another man, thunder-stricken like St. Paul, would perhaps have revised his premises; not so the unrepentant cleric. What he did was to alter his conclusions, modulate into a lighter key, frankly contradict himself, and take pleasure in bewildering his readers.

Friendly critics have described this decline from the serious to the merely amusing as " M. Renan's third manner." The first was learned and a trifle heavy, witness *Averroes*. The second, which took its color from Michelet and George Sand, was romantic, sentimental, persuasive, balanced, not incapable of rising to heights where the grandest historians had trodden. What was the third? In diction, admirably French, on a model that cannot quite be found under Louis Quatorze, yet is hinted by Fénelon, and would have been praised by Port Royal. The lucid words, however, and the sentences that flow like a stream of honey, do not convey one uniform or consistent idea. That charming woman, Madame Alphonse Daudet, said in her gentle way of Renan, when he had

delivered his address on being received into the
French Academy, " No, he really has not the sentiment of affirmation." He was the newest Abelard, setting in parallel phrases the " Yea and
Nay " of a spirit essentially incoherent.

He would not bribe the judge; that had been
his argument; but in things which lie outside
mathematics there is no judge, if we do not pass
sentence ourselves. What is Truth, if not sacred,
ethical, and the reward of conviction—in other
words, an active insight to which we contribute
all our powers, including a good will? At any
rate, we may watch this fine intellect losing its
grasp on reality in proportion as it loses its moral
earnestness. The unity of its conception wavers
and disappears; the Divine drama moves " in a
wide sea of wax," not tending anywhither; and
by a fortune which we have illustrated elsewhere
from his French contemporaries, this Plato becomes, instead of a noble thinker, a student in
bric-à-brac, idly strolling through collections wherever old curiosities are to be found. If science did
not lay down conclusions, why should he? The
plausible guesses which left events undecided—
much as certain story-tellers have written two end-
ings to their novels—were at least amusing. History thus became anecdotage, or psychology taught
by examples; the governing idea withdrew into its

own heaven whither no man could pursue it. Science, admitting its failure to interpret the facts, was yet a chapter, nay the whole series of chapters in the world's development which had been denominated "history" and "reason." The contradictions in such a view are flagrant enough; Renan assures us that they are inevitable and do not signify.

There is no room, and little need, to travel over the second Christian century with a guide so capricious. Yet we may remark on the comparative soundness of his judgment where it touches the Gospels, their date and their relation to one another, while the leading German critics were still at play among unverified conjectures. Questions remain which can be solved by no ingenuity, for the terms of a solution are not given. But in coming back toward the traditional view of the Synoptics, the Acts, the Pauline Epistles, Renan showed courage no less than acuteness, which deserve to be acknowledged. Of the Fourth Gospel he writes, after much hesitation, " It is likely that a disciple of the Apostle John, who had inherited many of his reminiscences, felt authorized to speak in his name, and twenty-five or thirty years after his death to write down those things which unhappily had not been fixed on paper during his lifetime." That Gospel was the stroke which at last

Rosmapamon.

delivered the Church from Judaism. It opened the way to Christian philosophy, as St. Paul had been the first to sketch its theology. But the canon of Scripture, to whom was that owing? Renan takes us to the year 180 A.D., to the Roman Church, and the Muratorian Fragment (since, in its original form, assigned to Hippolytus of Porto) as the time and place where the New Testament was closed against additions. His early admiration of Rome never died out. The Catholic Church, he declared, was the saving of Christianity from Gnostics, Oriental and Greek, who would have turned it with a host of wild fancies into a conventicle of madmen. And Rome first uttered that august name.

True, he continues with transcendent scorn, authority is founded on the commonplace; but bishops were preferable to epileptics, and in the Roman See bishops had a centre upon which they might always fall back. Not personal inspiration but collective wisdom; not anarchy but unity; this was the creative idea which became visible in Clement, and which, gaining power with every success, drawing to it appeals from orthodox and heretic, in the capital of the world, formed the keystone of an arch that would otherwise have fallen into a heap of ruins. The reconciliation of Peter and Paul in the Roman legend had been a master-stroke. Tradition, authority, prestige, were combining to establish the Papal dominion, which before the second century ended was manifest in sovereign acts, as when Victor threatened to excommunicate the Churches of Asia, though they pleaded against him St. John's example in the Quartodeciman controversy.

On questions like these, once hotly debated, but now in course of settlement, Renan was almost as Catholic as ever he had been. He could not trace in the Gnostic aberrations, which mingled with some elements of the Gospel fantastic and too often demoralizing myths from Asia Minor, nay from the Inner East, the true lines upon which Christian development moved. He had never taken the view, long favored by English and German historians, that, when the last of the Apostles died, a sudden lapse into Paganism followed, infecting the visible Church, and leaving only a hidden remnant who, by ways hardly discernible, continued through heretics like the Paulicians to hand on the saving Faith. He granted much—too much, it will be said by careful critics—not to this early Protestant reading of history, but to those who saw in Gnostic ritual, art and speculation the Church turned Pagan, accommodating itself to the heathen world, and, like all-conquering Rome, subdued by the Greeks. But still it *was* the Church, rooted and founded in the new Testament, which inherited from Jesus the Divine fire that burned in its Holy Place; from Peter its royal supremacy; from Paul and James and Luke its Sacraments in their primitive form, and its episcopal order; from John its rite of perpetual sacrifice, shadowed forth in the Apocalypse, and yet again its Logos, to whom all wisdom, Greek as well as Hebrew, must be ascribed.

By the *charismata* of unauthorized inspirations, he argued, no Church could have held together. Rome, with its genius for ruling over chaos by hierarchy, sacraments, synods, and public creeds, has tamed religious rebels or cast them out, chosen between the good and evil in Hellenic learning, and made the Christian State possible. This was not the corruption of the best; it was the reconciliation in thought and practice of all that mankind had brought down on innumerable lines out of a past which could never be recalled.

Nero had seen the growing power and striven to consume it on a funeral pile; he was the Antichrist by his triumphant and enormous vices. A hundred years later came Marcus Aurelius, saint and emperor, who was taught the sum of virtuous living by his father Antoninus, but who, on this very account, appears in Renan's last volume to be the rival of Jesus. Wholly independent of dogma, revelation, and the supernatural, he is lay virtue personified. These words, lay and clerical, which exert on French politics a charm not less deadly than the words Guelf and Ghibelline exerted on Italian cities in the time of Dante, suppose that men must be ranged in two hostile camps. The laic is a votary of Reason, self-sprung and self-sufficient; he is a humanitarian who believes in no God, and whose religion is social service. But he is likewise the unsleeping enemy of all who do not sign his creed. In his eyes every true disciple of Jesus is a traitor to civilization. "Lay" virtue breeds Jacobins; it shuts up Christian schools; it puts down religious orders; it sends priests and nuns to the guillotine, as in 1794. It is, in fine, a Church militant, with Inquisition, secular arm, cord, stake, and axe, for all those on whom it fixes the charge of *incivisme* or disbelief in its dogmas.

Renan, to his credit be it spoken, always defended the right of free association, which is in France cruelly hampered, and which in the case of Catholics has been over and over again suppressed. He could not bring himself to apologize for the old Roman Law, whose jealousy of private gatherings the French jurist had copied only too well. Yet, when he came to Marcus Aurelius, who in his own person embodied that Law, the temptation to set him up as the Christ of Rationalism proved too strong for Renan's principles, and with surprise we listen while a veteran among Liberals pours out his eulogy of absolute power. We call to mind other pages that implore France to have done with Roman jurisprudence, to learn from the free Barbarians what liberty can achieve for a nation; and now we are told that the Stoics founded that " Law of modern peoples " which is winning its triumph, slow but sure, over the Christian ideas. The Stoic, in Renan's account of him, is not to be distinguished from those French—*energumens* did he not style them once?—who, out of their seething caldron, would have drawn a regenerated country, but could evoke only phantasmal horrors. Making allowance for the complexities of a vast subject, in which the point of view changes with its field, we are still at a loss to imagine how the author would reconcile his love of freedom, which we cannot deny, with his admiration for a Law that never suffered it to breathe.

However, the contrast between Marcus, who wrote his own Gospel, and Another whose writing was the Cross, affords such a theme as grandly to sum up the long debate of Church and Empire, if not to bring about a reconciliation in which reason and faith might embrace. The manner of this concluding volume is exceedingly fine wherever it

touches on the *Meditations,* that sad and subduing book, not rightly termed by Renan the *Lay-
man's Vade Mecum,* for all its grace flows from
submission to the Divine Will, as revealed in the
nature of things. Marcus would not have made
common cause with Renan, though Renan strives
to be at one with Marcus. What fellowship has
the Stoic with the dilettante? Who could be less
of a Puritan than our sauntering professor, led by
a " lively curiosity," as he tells us, to consider the
ways of men? And who could be more so than
the Emperor, absorbed in his own spirit, eaten
up with scruples, always alone, sighing like a Christian saint over the perversity of human nature?

At this distance from Renan's novitiate we feel
that his fears, long ago expressed to the Abbé
Cognat, were by no means unfounded. " Even so,
could I be sure of myself! " he had written in
1845; " but how if I came to lose by contact with
them "—he means with irreverent Liberals—" the
purity of my heart and my view of life?—if they
succeeded in infecting me with their own Positiv-
ism? Who can know himself and not be afraid
of his weakness? " Intellectual weakness, which
staggers to and fro like a drunken man from one
view to its opposite; moral weakness, which cannot discern the Stoic who is hard upon himself
from the Jacobin who keeps all his austerity for

others; and, it must be said, even weakness, in the handling of art, since it betrayed the artist into a comparison which exalts the Roman Emperor, who founded nothing durable, above Christ and His Apostles, to whom mankind owes its salvation.

The drift of that specious argument is clear. For the last time Renan was contending on behalf of his Utopia which refused to be born. The advent of science, or lay knowledge, leading up to a philosophy in the shape of ethics founded on experience, without sanction from God or hope of Heaven, was to have brought in a social Paradise. How differently had things turned out! Wars and Rebellions; a burning Paris; a Republic of all the mediocrities; a sensible decline from heroism to money-making; and " a fall in ethical values," which portended misfortune still greater. Was, then, the supernatural justified by facts? He would never believe it. He pointed to the Roman Law which had given to Europe a golden age; he instanced the philanthropy of Marcus Aurelius, who was tender to slaves, orphans, and the helpless, though he persecuted Christians. After all, what need was there of Revelation?

Such is the lesson which this delicately wrought lay sermon inculcates through its six hundred pages. A fruitful essay might be attempted by one who should examine it with Pater's romance,

Marius the Epicurean, lying before him as a statement on the other side, equal to it in dainty phrasing, temperate and calm, but more in earnest, and in its conclusions more like the course of history. For while the unhappy Emperor, " animal infelicissima," could make martyrs at Lyons and Vienne, he could not put down the gladiatorial shows, or by his philosophy prevent his subjects from being dedicated in blood to Mithras, or purify the innumerable superstitions to which Apuleius, who knew them all intimately, bears witness. He might have been a blameless Constantine; he was in fact, but a nobler Julian, proving by his own example how little the Stoic reason can influence multitudes, and how barren was the lay reform on which he had set his heart.

But those Christians, we hear from Renan, who is almost as indignant as the heathen writers he is copying, bled the Empire to death by their determination not to mix in its business or its pleasures. Yet how could that be, if the Empire had a vitality which its Law sustained? In granting so much—and he repeats the charge when he is dealing with French Catholics—surely he is giving up his case. It would appear, then, that neither ancient philosophy nor modern science can furnish an enduring foundation for society. The Roman Empire fell because it accepted the Gospel too late in its career; the world is now rocked by revolutions because it has substituted for that Gospel a law which has no deeper sanction than use and wont. After the Antonines, Pagan Rome lost its justification to the moral sense. Christianity triumphed, for it had in it the promise of the world to come.

CHAPTER VII

ECCLESIASTES, OR THE PREACHER

SCEPTIC, idealist, amused spectator of all time and all existence—these provoking but not contradictory epithets paint the Renan who, between 1871 and 1892, disputed first with Victor Hugo and then with M. de Lesseps the distinction, whatever it was worth, of being the foremost French celebrity. In his own thought he was an Ecclesiastes, gay but without illusions, holding all things to be vanity, yet enjoying them as if they had savor and substance. His *Philosophic Dialogues* date back, as we saw, to Versailles and the agony of the Commune in 1871; they were varnished, so to call it, for publication in 1875. They begin somewhat like the *Decameron* during a season of distress, to end ironically in dreams that are set down by the dreamer as falsehoods which might hereafter come true. Thanks to his " third manner," one lobe of the brain might argue for the affirmative, while another maintained the negative. The play was to be rounded off with a smile and a sleep; for how could the preacher dogmatize if he had no settled beliefs, and who would take his word as peremptory? Dialogue, not dogma, was the new form of assertion; all systems in succession, or, better still, all at once. Yet the general effect was so unpleasant that a lady to whom Renan showed his manuscript exclaimed, " Do not print those pages; they make one's heart freeze."

Of course he did print them. He could revise endlessly what he had written; he seems never to have destroyed any of it. " I am not acquainted with a gay philosophy," said this stroller in Vanity Fair, beginning his discourse; but why not cultivate good humor, the best of all philosophies? Nature was herself eternally young. We had, indeed, come to a crisis without way of escape, unless she should invent one, as she had always done hitherto. The old doctrines which helped men to be virtuous had been rudely disturbed, and no others had taken their place. Idealism would suffice for the cultivated, who by instinct were well behaved, after the fashion of those creatures that went on acting as if alive when their brains had been removed. For the millions it was certainly not enough.

Such was the text of Renan's preachment to an unbelieving France. Had Père de Monsabré delivered it from the pulpit of Notre Dame, the hosts of anti-clericalism would have been up in arms against its cruel satire. But, however else he swung to and fro, on this chief point of a moral decadence Renan did not change. The outrages on good taste in his dramas, *The Water of Youth* and *The Abbess of Jouarre,* may be palliated, though not excused, by the strength of this conviction, which in very curious ways they illustrate. Renan was not only Ecclesiastes; the heterodox would have been warranted in calling him Balaam, for he blessed the tents of Jacob when desired to curse them altogether. He had known absolute virtue in his young days at Tréguier and Issy; the brilliant heathens with whom he dined in the Café Bréhant could never, he told them, imagine what it was like.

His " certitudes, probabilities, and guesses " acquaint the reader with nothing new. Nature is immoral; to justify the ways of God to men is a hopeless undertaking; abstract logic fails to show that He exists, and experience has never made Him known; but the heart reveals a category of the ideal, and why not be satisfied? Why not? we rejoin. Because the lay preacher is himself not satisfied. Take the proof.

Writing to M. Berthelot, in the letter that George Eliot slighted, Renan moves from this " pure idea " to an evolution, a world-making, so comprehensive that it swallows up history in the physics of the sun, and stretches out beyond our widest human advance to an indefinite future. Renan affirms that Deity is not yet, but shall be; and, while he denies intelligence and moral attributes to the First Cause, this eternal process, he believes, will bring forth a God of goodness and mercy at the end. No more glaring contradiction to his own thought and to the nature of things was ever ventured upon than is here proposed. The real is not the ideal, says our teacher, but a vast outrage on it, and history a series of defeats for the righteous; which if you grant, he will at once turn round upon you and prove that an ideal, an inward teleology as the Germans call it, is guiding the universe along paths which cannot but issue in such a millennium as the Prophets of Israel foresaw.

That Mr. Spencer should have held this creed was sufficiently astonishing; but he, at all events, did not oppose history to science, and both to philosophy, by way of premises to a scheme from which evil disappears. If the Idea is not revealed in Nature, where can it be found? And if it governs Nature, how is it not revealed? Renan puts the question to himself, " How reconcile such sentiments "—as universal benevolence—" with an iron law of things, with belief in the sovereign rule of reason?" He replies, " I do not know, and I care as little. Benevolence does not depend on theory." With a fervor not quite reassuring he continues, " One thing is certain, Humanity will draw from its own heart as many illusions as it requires to fulfil its duties and accomplish its destiny. It has not failed hitherto, nor will it fail." In other words, it can always be deceived by itself.

The cynic has had his jest; the dreamer follows it up. We may imagine the unity toward which all things are moving as a sensorium or " conscience "—to use the French expression—and this again as shared by many, or by few, or appropriated to himself by a single individual. Science will surely be master of this planet; or, should earth perish in a catastrophe of the solar system, then of some other. Will democracy prevail in that ordered world? It is not likely, answers Théoctiste; culture, discipline, progress, are incompatible with an American suffrage. The leveller is condemned by Nature and Darwin. But might there not come to pass a rule of the select, armed with all-creating, all-annihilating knowledge, irresistible as no Church or State ever was? A senate of gods would then dominate mankind. Lastly, however, an omnipotent biologist, emerging from his equals, might concentrate in a life without end pleasure, wisdom and goodness, while the few and the many, absorbed in that great whole, would enjoy " by procuration " their share of the universe. Some one has called this the " monstrous image of an infinite beast." Happily! But now a pantheistic vision, not without resemblance to the *Bhagavat Gita,* though wanting its tender pity, closes the scene. Is it a vision of Something or of Nothing? The seer himself could not tell; nor can we.

Style is Renan's unfailing miracle. By their cunning design, bold excursions into Chaos, attacks on vulgar democracy, and even by their sadness, the *Dialogues* won fresh glory for the dissident from every school. But when he talked of his " omnipotent biologist " in the hearing of men like Théophile Gautier, Homeric laughter greeted him, nor could he help joining in it. The old metaphysicians, it would seem, were not so grotesque in their wild flights as the latest amateur of science. Before many years they were to take their revenge. By and by Renan would be saying, " Let us not make haste to arrive at the Truth. Who knows whether it may not be something melancholy? " The former dogmatist, who had put his faith in religion only to renounce it, now went away sad from the oracle of science after giving it a trial. He wrapped himself round in illusion, took the most comfortable stall in the theatre, and gently applauded until, for him at any rate, the play was played out. M. Séailles pictures him as one that, from his days at the seminary, had " lived in a mental intoxication." It is very well said, and for an epigram it is true. Curiosity, observed Renan, reflecting on his own tastes, will be always an entertainment, even if this world should turn out to be nothing but the dream of a sickly God.

For a moment, however, in these *Dialogues* he put on the sable cloak of Schopenhauer. He did what in him lay to be discontented with existence and to rail at the Supreme. But the iron had not entered deep enough into his soul. A man who prospered evermore as years went on, whose versatility afforded him boundless amusement, and whose public was the whole of educated Europe, admiring even when it was most critical, must have been haughtier than Diogenes if he did not enjoy the sunshine which his Alexander allowed him.

Travel was always his delight. In 1874 he took his wife to Lugano, Venice, Mantua. A year later, in August, 1875, he visited Sicily, attending the scientific congress at Palermo and racing, as he said, in a headlong course over the island, being everywhere received with speeches and what the newspapers call ovations. He took it all very kindly. The clergy themselves were polite to him, and science won their applause. From Messina he went on to Naples, making pleased acquaintance with Ischia, the charming islet of this self-styled Prospero, where he spent several of his summer holidays. Famous but rheumatic, middle-aged yet growing light-hearted, he delivered at Amsterdam in 1877 the commemorative address on Spinoza. Next year he visited Constance, Innsbruck, and Venice. From Florence he despatched a curious letter to Berthelot, in which he tells his friend that the rivalry of nations will prove not less mischievous than did in former times the intrigues of dynasties; that patriotism after this fashion will not last fifty years; and that all is vanity except science. " Even art," he concludes, " begins to seem rather empty. My impressions of twenty-five years ago have a touch of childishness on them. At the point of view that we have attained, no picture can teach us anything. In short, these things were once living, and that must suffice."

Persevering, not to say ambitious, he had become member of the French Institute, Hebrew professor, an author second to none, by sheer hard work, tact and daring, and by a politic though not servile attendance on the chiefs in these various departments. He knew everybody that was worth knowing in Paris. He served the Collège de France with zeal tempered by discretion, and was much liked for his invariable kindness, which did not prevent him from being firm or even unyielding on the fit occasion. His courtesy, which he attributes to St. Sulpice, made him a flatterer in conversation, whatever the subject, provided that certain views of his own were not assailed. For Renan had his prejudices, and only the simpleminded were taken in by his favorite expression, " Vous avez mille fois raison, Monsieur." He greatly disliked the reigning schools of literature and painting in France; but his opposition was not violent, though it grew rather than diminished as the ugly Realist flaunted his glaring or unclean exhibitions at every salon and on every bookstall, with shameless impudence.

Praising the bewigged seventeenth century, setting up Cousin for a model of grace and measure when affectation was the order of the day, this literary Girondin gave intolerable offence to Goncourt, Gautier, Zola—men in their several ways Jacobins who would have guillotined Louis Quatorze. By instinct he had felt long ago that to speak with commendation of Port Royal and the Jansenists was excellent policy. He did so, yet what could be less to his liking than the sadbrowed features of Pascal, or St. Cyran's cast-iron dogmas? Now he had his reward. Among his friends who leaned to that sterner view was M. de Sacy, son of the well-known Oriental scholar. And to the influence of this gentle Jansenist, as we learn, he owed the decorated coat which all French men of letters rate as highly as English dukes rate the Garter. On April 3, 1879, he read himself into the French Academy.

Believers were scandalized at this public recognition of a man whose talents had been spent in undermining the Gospel. Dupanloup, Bishop of Orleans, and his early benefactor, gave up his chair as an Academician. There was an outcry almost as loud as when the *Life of Jesus* had first appeared. But honors, in a Republic now decidedly turning from the tolerant traditions of 1848 to Secularist principles, were destined for men who, like Renan, could give it lustre by their adhesion, however qualified. His nomination to the Academy was among the spoils torn from Conservatives on that fatal Sixteenth of May, which marked the last failure of the Bourbons to conquer France. He was no democrat. But in the motley array of opponents to ancient Christendom, to priest, altar, and revelation, he bore a standard, far-shining as it moved. No one could mistake its device, few as they might be who were able to read it distinctly.

An air of supreme satisfaction, which only just escapes the note of fatuity, reigns over his inaugural address from the arm-chair lately occupied by Claude Bernard. It is a custom which often leads to situations trying or ludicrous that the new Academician shall praise the deceased who has obligingly made way for him. That duty Renan fulfilled in a speech of singular dexterity, in a style clear and strong, adapted to the subject, while he was more than commonly moved by a career which, beginning like his own, in poverty, had been exposed to trials far longer. He made light of Bernard's confusion in thought when that Æsculapius attempted to pass beyond experiment and fell into a sort of metaphysics. The well-worn axioms of Renan's Hegelian system danced their minuet once more; contradiction the mother of truth; morals a lighthouse with revolving signals; the ideal and the real, spheres that do not touch; yet we are invited to conclude that infinite benevolence made the world and guides it onward.

Can we be surprised if plain men and acute women found this whirlwind of atoms rather provoking? Renan sighed over the severity of human creatures toward one another. He was not apologizing for what he had written; yet to those who possess the "sentiment of affirmation," as Madame Daudet so admirably termed it, this nerve-

less, effeminate resolution of all truths into the
vague, must have appeared more dangerous than
the *Life of Jesus* itself. It was indifference cultivated as a fine art; and how could nations or individuals live on such a Yea and Nay? Voltaire,
in comparison, was tonic. But Voltaire's eyes
would have gleamed when, with delicate mockery,
the new member told his associates that even in
their delays they were just. "One arrives in your
assembly," said he, "at the age of Ecclesiastes, a
charming age, most proper to serene cheerfulness,
when, after laborious youth, one begins to perceive
that all is vanity, but that many a vain thing ought
to be thoroughly enjoyed."

He prided himself on being a very clubable man.
Such, in fact, he was. Good nature sustained by
success, philosophic disdain, and nerves not irri-
tated by his dedication to scholarship, made him
welcome at every meeting of the Forty, a guest
much sought after in drawing-rooms. He was, in
short, Caliban to look upon, but Ariel when he
opened his lips.

Not without a sense of mischief, he drew attention to the contrast between his genius and his outward man which, at every turn, gave so peculiar
an attraction to what he said and did. He became his own jester, shaking his bells and cracking
his whip about him gracefully. He called himself

" un prêtre manqué," whom the secular dress
would never fit. The public did its best to spoil
Renan; but he, though playing down to it like a
finished actor, kept in ironical reserve the principles that he had long ago enunciated. Great writers, it had been said, could only deal with the
public as if it were a child; not so, he replied,
you must deal with it as a woman. His method
was, in appearance, flattering; but we may be sure
that when he sparkled, and smiled, and, in a glit-
tering phrase, denied the existence of evil, he was
throwing into his part a dramatic fervor that vanished as soon as the curtain fell. Unlike Voltaire
in so many ways, he was like him thus far; the
habit of persiflage alternated with a real and deep
sense of insecurity before the unknown. Victor
Hugo might have labelled Renan, during his last
twelve or fourteen years, as " l'homme qui rit ";
it became his rubric, his *Leitmotif;* and, certainly,
a moral dissolution was setting in.

If we have not marked his three stages already,
let us mark them now. Religion, founded on reasoning, had passed away; science could not establish the moral order; perhaps the frivolous were
in the right. God, the soul, virtue, were " good
old words, rather heavy-sided," which men might
use until they invented better. To be sure about
them was to proclaim oneself a possible dupe.

When Pasteur, who took them seriously, ventured to hope that among the French Academicians they might still claim a refuge, Renan warned him that he was expecting too much. Pasteur said, in his devout, scientific way, " He that affirms the infinite, heaps up in that statement more of the supernatural than all the miracles of all religions." His polite but inflexible adversary answered, " You go too far, Monsieur." Littré, whom Pasteur succeeded (and who died a Christian), had shown that miracles do not happen. But Littré, he granted, was resigned to the inexorable laws of Nature; while Renan looked upon death as an outrage, philosophy as a deception, and could not lay aside these bitter thoughts.

To console himself, he fell back on his recollection of the days that were no more. He would write his *Reminiscences of Youth.* Moreover, could he not, by means of a volatile spirit, evaporate into dramas the philosophical *Dialogues,* where all things might be hinted but nothing affirmed? And since he had explained how Christianity sprang up, without calling on any but natural influences to account for it, there was the History of Israel awaiting his hand, to be dealt with on similar terms. These exercises did not fill up all his days. In 1882 he was chosen President of the Asiatic Society; two years later he became Administrator of the Collège de France. He delivered amusing speeches at the Breton dinner, which was held near the railway-station of Mont Parnasse. He accepted an invitation from the Félibres, or Provençal Society. When the Prix Montyon were to be distributed, his allocution was in request. And at the breaking up of the Lycée Louis le Grand he bestowed their wreaths on the young competitors, with a speech wherein he undertook to refute the pessimism of Jouffroy and of the day, which was always threatening to refute his own philosophy and to justify religion.

Few events in a course now singularly smooth can have given him more pleasure than the proposal which he accepted from the Hibbert trustees to lecture at Langham Place in April, 1880. He crossed the Channel, and found London somewhat like a " big village admirably clean and well kept," while he judged South Kensington to be the very pattern of an opulent city. The enlightened circles which opened their doors to him were the most charming in the world. Progress in England, he told Berthelot, was due to the upper classes, in great part Liberal; the masses were asleep; Church and State had no fear of attack. All this reminded him of the French eighteenth century before the Revolution. His own France, just then, was committing an " enormous offence " against the principles of freedom by driving out the religious orders, and Englishmen did not approve. M. Berthelot answered, not without asperity, that Englishmen were talking at their ease; if they ever had Jesuits to deal with again, they would be, as their foreign politics demonstrated, hard, brutal, and illiberal. But he admitted that Jules Ferry had not gone about his task in the right way.

Renan's lectures, which dwelt on the part taken by Rome in founding Christianity, were delivered to a choice audience, in accents so clear and in a French so classical, that no syllable of them could be lost. Their tone, considering where the lecturer stood, was perhaps a calculated irony. For they made much of the Petrine elements, the Papal tradition, and what we might describe as the Catholic influences, to which, in Renan's judgment, Christendom owed its lasting form. On these things whoever has dipped into his volumes will need no instruction. The Lectures are a pleasing mosaic, fragments not unskilfully taken from works already in print; but they hardly deserve a separate place among his writings as *Conferences in England.*

The " masses " took little heed of an unbeliever who could not speak their language. Max Müller asked him to Oxford, where he spent one Sunday. He was enchanted with all that he saw, though

compelled to hear a sermon in St. Mary's and to
be present at an "interminable evensong." His
reflections to Berthelot paint the man amusingly.
"Oh, the curious city!" he breaks out; "you must
really see it. It is the oddest relic of the past, the
type of death in life. Every college is an earthly
Paradise, but a Paradise forsaken. You would
say that life had gone elsewhere; but there is Paradise—planted, swept, weeded for those who have
left it. A poor outcome altogether; a mere hu-
manist and quite clerical training, given to a gilded
youth who attend choir in surplices; an utter absence of the scientific spirit. A college may possess a million (of francs) as yearly income; the
'fellows' succeed in proving that if they are to
keep their lawn in order, as the statutes oblige,
they must dispense with undergraduates, and they
spend the revenues hunting or shooting in all parts
of the world." He was alluding to All Souls;
but he did not suspect that Queen's College, a few
yards down the High Street, was then producing
an Assyrian scholar, whose *Light from the Monuments* would contribute with other English discoveries to make no small portion of his own *History
of Israel* obsolete in not many years.

His holidays and his seldom intermitted rheu-
matism, which was complicated by weakness of the
heart, took him to Plombières in the rainy August

of 1880. There he revised the *Water of Youth*, a sequel to *Caliban*, written in the frivolous vein which he mistook for humor and genius. We will touch upon it when we come to speak of his *Dramas*. He was also translating Ecclesiastes on a new plan; and that book, which many have thought among the saddest ever due to an inspired teacher, he discovered to be amiable and amusing. These are not precisely its qualities; but Renan, who could never forget himself, now saw his image and likeness in every work which he admired.

We need scarcely undertake to analyze his version of *Koheleth*, or to combat his Epicurean approval of a good sense which passed by the Law and the Prophets into its garden enclosed, there to enjoy life at leisure. But certain pages have attained great celebrity, as betokening the attitude which this veteran student of Hebraism took up toward the Israelite whom we now welcome within our gates.

Renan portrays, besides the enthusiast or fanatic who heads revolutions—Lassalle, Karl Marx, and their kind—the Sadducee, or man of the world, animated like his prophetic brother with unbounded confidence in himself—the mood called *tikva*, which is trust in destiny, insolent and unconquerable—yet careless about the coming of any

Messiah.   And in this triumphant money-changer,
who has inherited whatever his people could grasp,
Koheleth lives again.   He is pre-eminently the
" modern Jew."

Between him and Heinrich Heine, says Renan,
there is but a door to open.   After two thousand
years, behold him an accomplished worldling; he
has no prejudices, either feudal or dynastic; he
takes possession of a universe which he has not
made.   It is for him that Clovis and the Franks
have conquered.   He is, indeed, no democrat.   His
smooth skin, nervous susceptibility, scorn of man-
ual labor, make of him a noble; yet he is not given
to warlike feats.   Though he carries an air of
distinction, he can stoop to the ground; and therein
he stamps himself of the middle class.   Chivalry
and asceticism are alike far from him.   " He has
reached the perfect wisdom," concludes this por-
trait-painter in a half-mocking aside, " which is to
enjoy peacefully, amid works of delicate art and
images of exhausted pleasure, the fruit for which
he has labored.   Surprising proof that all is vanity!   Go to, then; trouble the world, compel your
God to expire on a cross, brave all tortures, set
your country on fire half-a-dozen times, insult
tyrants, throw down idols, that you may die of
spinal disease, in a luxurious mansion of the Champs
Élysées, lamenting that life is short and pleasure
fugitive.   Vanity of vanities!'

We have all come across that modern Jew, says Renan; he means in Paris, under the Third Republic. But was there not, in the critic whom we watch as he transforms himself into a tired satirist, more than one resemblance to Koheleth? Riches he did not seek, indeed. When Madame Renan talked anxiously of household cares, he answered, smiling, that money had never paid their house a call; and we may be sure that the volume he studied least was his bank-book. He professed to be a minor in worldly affairs, under the tutorship of M. Michel Lévy—Hebrew by his name—with whose rendering of accounts he never quarrelled. His ambition, from a child, had been to write; he did not imagine his thoughts could be sold in the market. His various appointments brought an income which, even when we add to it his literary gains, appears to have been much smaller than we should have argued from so immense a reputation. He did, of course, enjoy his modest comforts; he travelled for amusement; and in his last years he made a country-house of the Breton manor called Rosmapamon, close to delightful woods, down by the sea which his ancestors had so often sailed over. But he was never wealthy; and his likeness to the Israelite now in fashion must be looked for elsewhere.

When, then, he declares that for men such as

the " Preacher," no Messiah, no resurrection, no
patriotism held out a lure, whom is he describing
but himself, as books and conversations report
him? Who is it that " ought to be impious," if
he obeyed his own logic, but is " touchingly inconsequent," and on the brink of Materialism draws
back? Who is the amiable sceptic, the resigned
Schopenhauer, so much beyond the hero of German drinking-bouts, the reasoner that will not
cleave superstitiously to any inference, the man
that loves life though he sees through it, and is
an exquisite person with manners which one cannot resist? Where should we seek him that " could
not be led astray by the delusion of the supernatural "; that was " supple yet proud toward the
powers that be "; that scorned democracy because
he held by heredity, and that detested conscrip-
tion, the barracks, the battle-field? Who, again,
could work, and enjoy, and expect no to-morrow,
and find his Heaven in the beautiful things of
which the world was full? Whether such a one
answers to the name of Solomon, or Heine, or
Renan, we know him to be a disenchanted idealist,
whose voice, if it sounded alone, would be fatal to
the best that is in us.

But the sceptic lives on a capital stored up
during the days when he believed. He is a philosopher on half-pay. All that makes Renan at-

tractive came to him from his ancestors in Brittany, his teachers in St. Sulpice, while the never-
ending debate between ideals which he knew not
how to reconcile—a debate carried on in public
by this accomplished tragi-comedian—threw over
each of his volumes the uncertainty that men hate
in life, but find entertaining in literature. At the
stage where he now was, keeping, as he remarked,
a system by double entry, to teach straight on had
grown impossible. He could only exchange confidences with his readers, talk of old times, gently
criticise when the Republicans indulged their ap-
petite for adventure in Tunis or Tonquin, and give
his *Reminiscences* to the thousands who had seldom travelled farther in their exploration of him
than extracts from his most notorious volume
would permit. Autobiography is fascinating, and
here was a past master in the craft, though always
on his own terms.

The *Reminiscences of My Youth* appeared as a
complete book in 1883. " A race," he said afterward, " lives forever on its recollections of childhood." So he would live himself, and through
him the Bretons who were in him summed up as
their incarnate genius. This was his thought, almost his expression. No French biography, since
Chateaubriand published his *Memoirs from the
Tomb,* had created a stir equal to the sensation

which now followed. Twenty-two editions in half
the number of years did not exhaust a demand,
everywhere felt among the cultivated, for pages
that might justify Renan's admirers or accusers,
both eager to learn his secret.

A volume, indeed, of *Memoirs* as the word is
understood at Mudie's, Renan neither could nor
would have given them. For dates, scenes, incidents, the many-colored story which those who
have played great parts dress up, and leave to be
published twenty years after their funeral, he had
no taste. His education at the seminary made him
what he had proved to be as an historian, whether
he was rendering St. Paul, Marcus Aurelius, or
himself, in his faultless French. Always inter-
ested, and interesting, he was yet detached from
his subject. Now the virtue of detachment would
be fatal to Rousseau; it forbids self-portraiture
except from a religious point of view; and Renan
never had been, as the spiritual writers name it,
an interior man. He looked at the world with
his own eyes, but the vision was not directed to
feelings; it sought after facts as a clue to ideas.
Upon this moral quality the training which he
received in abstract systems, where philosophers
themselves appeared only as a set of syllogisms
to be sustained or demolished, could not fail to
react. And so the picturesque died out for want

Ernest Renan, 1892.
From the painting by Bonnat

of color, and that which M. Bourget has well termed the violent energy of life was exhausted by an asceticism of the imagination far more effective than hair-shirt or knotted cords would have been.

From that medium Renan, though struggling valiantly, never got quite free. Though others could not have written about his first years unless he had shown the way, we must agree with Turgenieff that he was never meant for a story-teller. He was, indeed, a being apart. Many Liberals felt it and did not like him; the orthodox were sensible of it in another way—they shuddered as at an apostate priest. He knew himself how little he could compete with genuine poets, with Alfred de Musset, for example, who is here suggested by force of contrast, or with Heine, who was much too sensuous ever to be a Koheleth meditating upon the fatal sameness of things.

Thus the *Reminiscences* are not psychology, as are Rousseau's *Confessions*. But they give the history of an idea. Calm, with a tranquillity born of science, to which persons only stand for symbols, not for beating hearts and passionate ecstasies of joy or sorrow, they tell how the Christian became an unbeliever, and in the voice we catch no sound of tears. "A curious experience," the writer seems to say, "of which I happened to be the subject." He dissects a corpse that had once, in some previous avatar, been animated by his own soul. This high impersonality, shocking to the devout, is proper in a dissecting-room. And it would be superfluous to imagine that Renan kept back any part of the demonstration, so far as he had made it. However mistaken, he was surely sincere. If we grant that moral issues ought to be decided by methods like these, all the anguish, fear, and poignant grief which have accompanied spiritual wrestlings in other men, who dreaded lest they should lose their immortal treasure, may be put aside; they are unscientific. The problem of eternity is seen to be a question for grammarians; not "What shall I do to be saved?" but "How do I read?" sums up and shapes the whole controversy.

Plausible as such a method appears—for is it not objective and impartial?—the deeper sense of mankind refuses to act upon it. Men will go by custom, inspiration, example—nay, by simple guess-work—rather than trust themselves to the "small conjectural sciences," which, according to Renan, make our books of history and are themselves unmade in the process. "The regret of my life," he writes, "is that I chose to engage in researches which never can be certified; which must ever turn on interesting considerations about a vanished reality." The world, he thinks, will in a hundred years be forgetting its past. Do we want to know the secret of existence? Let us consult astronomy and general physiology, and exchange the prophets for Darwin. How we are to establish on a doctrine of evolution thus restricted, any morals but those of profit and loss in view of the species, we shall not learn from our teacher. But yet we know that the ideals of life must somehow find their justification; and is not this sufficient evidence that he has taken the wrong path?

His *Reminiscences,* which begin so romantically, and yet are not a fiction, would possess little charm had his scientific method been a true one. It is the soul for which we are concerned; the experiment is fraught with issues beyond the ken of star-gazers and general physiologists. When he enters the lodge at Issy of " la Reine Margot," he bears in his heart something which dies before he leaves it again, or which he murders—his faith, which had lighted up the unseen and made it visible as a divine world. However it comes about, he is by that loss everlastingly poor; though he should exclaim, as he does, with the Italian poet, that to be wrecked in such an ocean is pleasant to him. The shipwreck cannot be denied; henceforth he floats on a raft, made from its drifting spars. He is resigned, but still he floats, without a compass, over seas that promise him no haven.

We cannot, then, forbear to agree with M. Séailles when he tells us that " The history of one who was among the brilliant intellects of our time leaves a profound impression of sadness. From the heroism of the stripling, as he throws himself resolutely into the life of thought; from his high ambitions when he composed the *Future of Science,* impatient to conquer the truth which sounded for him alone its proud flourish of trumpets, to the submission of old age, defeated by life, finding pleasure in its very abasement, the fall is great indeed. That Renan should have been understood, accepted, flattered, only when he fell, can make no difference. Let who will admire this vacillating mind, this impotence to affirm, we know it to be the last term of decadence."

No one who feels kindly toward an amiable spirit, or who has found pleasure in his captivating ways of speech, but will be grieved on assenting to this judgment. Its truth may be hidden for many readers, seeking as they do literary entertainment at the cost of tragedy, and delighted with Renan's myrtle and jessamine, while he takes them round his perfumed garden. But even the enchanted ass of Apuleius could not feed exclusively on roses. It would seem that eternal life must

be bought at a higher price. The awkward pen-
sive student holds us by the heartstrings; when he
gives up his vocation, we suffer with him as in a
catastrophe where the whole man succumbs. But
for the amused spectator of his own early strug-
gles, we are affected with a sense of pity not altogether free from disdain. He has grasped at
everything and taken nothing. Yet he does not
perceive that his hands are empty.

Chateaubriand, with gifts more extraordinary,
was a dissolute rhetorician; his *Memoirs,* though
superb in style, cannot furnish the comparison we
are seeking by which to estimate a more modest,
not a less important, biography. If character be
our aim, we might lay these *Reminiscences* not far
from the *Words of a Believer,* and dwell on the
fiery zeal which devoured Lamennais, the calm serenity which tones down or effaces in Renan colors
that had never been overcharged. The hackneyed
word *la nuance,* or shading, rises to our lips when
we contrast his subdued atmosphere with a light
so strong that it blinds its adorer. But character
is rooted in principle, and the key to it is conscience. Let us ask again, therefore, do we feel
that conscience is but the echo of our own voice,
or is the voice of God to which we must hearken?
All, we may truly say, lies there, in that first and
deepest of distinctions. To judge the defence of

himself which Renan puts forward, let us take another and an opposite, the *Apologia* of Cardinal Newman.

The difference goes deeper than logic; it is not exhausted by writing in the margin "temperament"; for it holds of reason, will, and whatever else is our innermost, our real self. To Newman the world outside him brought no message until he had interpreted its lines from within. He construed it in terms of personality, yet not simply his own; experience revealed to him one which possessed the attributes of Justice and Holiness, which was in the highest degree living and the law of all things. But this inward vision it does not appear that Renan ever enjoyed. Amazing as the affirmation sounds to us, he came to believe that no mind greater than the human existed anywhere. To him, therefore, the moral law was an acquisition, not from a Divine source, but as literally manufactured as the Code Napoléon by civic wisdom. Prayer, when there is none to listen, cannot profit much; and so far from the thinker being less than the universe, he is its superior, urging it forward to a perfection it could never reach were he not driving it, the only Phœbus Apollo in his chariot of the sun. What, then, is religion? It is worship of the higher, ideal self. What is conscience? Surely the dream of a shade. It can

never be the voice of a God who has not yet begun
to be. Man is not "alone with the Alone," he
is alone with himself.

Hence the passionate pilgrimage of Newman
goes by prayer and self-discipline, along the way
of the cross, to a truth which is ever becoming
more of a service, and which ends in a concrete,
historical revelation. The *Apologia* is likewise a
Theodicæa; truly, it justifies the ways of God to
men. It vindicates the Christian creed by showing
how we may live on its teaching. The conclusion
is highly practical, instant, not to be mistaken. In
the rudest of language it would be convincing; in
the most refined it cannot be more. The light thus
gained opens a view into eternity; it is the seed
which yields a harvest, and is equal to endless
developments. It restores the inward sense of
things; it accounts for the least by the greatest
as due to an all-encompassing design. Having
overcome the sting of death, it looks forward in
hope to life without end. And this would be, to
a scientific mind, its justification.

Renan, when he ceases to be a pilgrim, can hope
no longer. He commits progress to the infinite
of hazard, which from Epicurus to our own day
has taken the dice-box and all it contains for
granted. But who can tell, he inquires elsewhere,
if the capital of which Nature disposes may not

run out? Thus, said a French wit, he leaves his ideal at the mercy of the coal-measures. To sum up: if chance reigns, how shall we prophesy? And if it does not, where can reason pause until it grants creative Intelligence?

CHAPTER VIII

LAST DAYS, DEATH, AND EPITAPH

SUCH were the notes of interrogation which Renan might have scattered over his unpretending and, to so many, delightful little book. It is easy to read; we shall not, however, learn its meaning if we sunder it from his philosophic dialogues and dramas, or his frequent soliloquies, which round it off in unexpected fashion. These are commonly bitter-sweet; while the *Reminiscences* put on the tone of good society, and are gay and genial. At no time could Renan appropriate to himself " the diabolic lucidity of Voltaire, the devouring flame of Diderot." He was incapable of drawing scenes or showing his life in action. He did not observe in order to narrate; but he took a moral impression which passed over costume, figure, attitude, and all that makes a picture as not to his purpose. Landscape he saw and loved. For people he had not the eye of a painter, though he knew, none better, how they stood to him and he to them. Hence the *Reminiscences* are written in a key of sentiment, not of color; and thus we learn why they were eagerly read, like the *Life of Jesus,* by many women; for in literature sentiment is Eve's Paradise, where she listens to the serpent.

Perhaps we have now arrived, by a way we were not looking for, at an explanation of the strangely elusive genius, who was, beyond question, more subtle than any freethinker among his contemporaries. When he is not scientific he becomes sentimental; these are the positive and negative poles round which the current of his being circulates. Sentiment defies analysis and laughs definition to scorn. It may clasp the universe, calling itself cosmic emotion; and in that mood Renan employs the language of piety which, in strict logic, he ought to have discarded. Again, it may frankly admit the limitations of physical science, turn from knowledge to passion, and write the *Abbess of Jouarre.* Instinct, long kept under, may claim its revenge. The laggard Cupid, says Madame Darmesteter, with an allusion to this last book, that flitted round the hammock in which Socrates lay philosophizing at fifty-three, provokes a smile. But did not Renan, with unwonted lack of civility, declare in his *Reminiscences* that " the more a man increases in understanding, so much the more does he seek rest at the opposite pole, in complete ignorance, or the woman who is nothing but herself "? He adds prettily, " The innocence of a child who knows not that she is beautiful, and who sees God clear as day, is the great revelation of the ideal."

So the wheel has turned round. He, the stern Jacob wrestling with God's angel, full of syllogisms and unpolished school-terms, confident that by questioning he could find a key to every door, talks like a mystic, and puts love instead of knowledge. True, the genuine mystic, at least if a Christian, denies himself earthly love that he may attain the heavenly; while with advancing years Renan bestowed a plenary indulgence on the faults of youth, in which he had never been entangled. Once he had spoken severely of the " Gallic spirit, vulgar, prosaic, without elevation, which understands morality as the art of getting on."   French laughter, French ballads, were his abomination; " prurient vice, coquettish impropriety, making evil attractive—look," he said, "there is the French sin *par excellence,* the absurdity which a Frenchman thinks to escape by his easy air and his eternal smile." He loathed Béranger, who was the poet of all these ineptitudes. " Let us remember," he had explained, " that sadness alone is the mother of great things!" The frivolous, the superficial man was the real atheist.

It has been well said that in Renan's earlier writings we may light upon the condemnation of whatever in his last days we should wish unwritten. Himself a rare example of hard work, sober, studious, moderate, decorous, whose life hid nothing of which he need be ashamed, he followed after the multitude, not to sin as they did, but in flowery phrases to condone their sinning. He affirmed, on this hand, that French democracy was "the most energetic dissolvent of virtue the world had ever seen." And on that he spoke an apology for intemperance, loose living, and the Caliban who personifies the triumphant Republic. "As a piece of satire, a showing up of the drunken Helot," we shall be told. Not in any way. Renan is quite serious. That he would not choose to live under the sway of Caliban we knew long ago; he made no secret of it. Republicans, when true to principle, are reformers; but he thinks the masses cannot be virtuous, and ought to be amused. Let them drink on their Saints' days, as in the *pardons* of Brittany. An intoxicated "Sabbat" is good enough for them.

This Caliban, with its sequel, *The Water of Youth*, leads up to a lugubrious but powerful imagination, *The Priest of Nemi*. Unless we turned to these dramas, we should hardly be aware of a certain skill which Renan possessed in dialogue; not the stage-repartee, but the cut and thrust of real ideas; neither should we be able fully to measure the " frightful incoherence " that a golden style elsewhere conceals.

He has made very free with Shakespeare. The quaint or exquisite creations of *The Tempest* are not to be looked for in scenes which border on pantomime, or in types so transparent that the abstract notion out of which they sprang could scarcely be more foreign to flesh and blood. One may conjecture that Renan was little versed in English books. He never quotes from them. He began, but could not go on reading Macaulay, whom Taine thought superior to most of our men of letters, while to M. Brunetière he seems our only prose classic. Shakespeare, then, may be left out of comparison, luckily for Renan. The plays are parables. Prospero is modern science, analytic and synthetic; Caliban represents drunken democracy; the Inquisitor, baffled by freedom of worship and unlicensed printing—we need not ask for whom he stands; while the musician, Ariel, is religion or Idealism. The stage, Milan, may be France, Paris, any centre of revolutionary strife. Prospero is dethroned on a gala-day by the people; Caliban—say Gambetta—seizes the vacant chair; and lo, the ruffian, to his own surprise, undergoes transformation. By instinct he turns Conservative. He guarantees private property, becomes a patron of the fine arts, enters into alliance with

Rome, which is ready to crown and consecrate him.
But Prospero, safe in his Certosa of Pavia, shall
not be made a holocaust. " Pardon's the word
for all." No, not for Ariel, who cannot breathe
in this dense medium, and who dies on a lingering
chord of his own music.

There is something bitter and not feigned in
Renan's contemptuous homage to a Government
which he and his aristocracy of talent could not
overthrow. He took leave to mock it as a thing
most brutish, praising with a cynic gesture its tol-
eration for such men as himself, the Prospero
whom a French Academy, founded by a Roman
cardinal, sheltered from the mob. Science had
permission to exist in the Republic, and, if it knew
how, was encouraged to compound an elixir of
life.

Not so did the Church reason in her palmy days,
according to the philosophic dramatist. The
Water of Youth transports us to Avignon, with
its famous bridge, palace, and French Pope, the
luxurious Clement VI. Prospero has been arrested
in the disguise of Arnold, a heretic and innovator,
whose distilling of magic liquors cannot but trouble good Christians. In spite of the enlightened
Clement, to say nothing of Brunissende—and the
less said of her the better—death is the penalty
of his too copious knowledge. Prospero, wiser

than Socrates, puts by the hemlock to quaff the elixir which brings him deliverance. He has invented a method of painless suicide, or, as the Greeks have it, *euthanasia*. The dying philosopher is consoled by love; Ariel revives, and, in his turn, consoles Cêlestine, a young person whom we need not describe, for she has little in common with Miranda. And the play finishes with dancing on the bridge of Avignon, where it began.

These doubtful satires, not altogether welcome in lay company, to which Renan appeared as a sort of priest, recall what he had written concerning Lamennais. They were " bold blasphemies," such as have been familiar at all times to apostates, and are characteristic of them. It was even said that he went beyond Voltaire, by transposing the language of devotion to antichristian uses. At all events, it is only in French literature that we come upon so sustained and deliberate a parody of holy things, the " flowers of evil " which a man grown aged by midnight lamps and studies should have refrained from planting. Was not this also vanity?

Fantasies, without the salt of life in them, miracle-plays dedicated to science, are among the *Senilia* which in a famous career we would willingly forget. *The Priest of Nemi* commands a deeper interest. It moves about Renan, its undoubted hero, and France in a period of eclipse, religious or political. Every one has heard the story as told in the *Lays of Ancient Rome*. A most learned and ingenious commentator, Mr. Frazer, has made of it, in his *Golden Bough*, the text on which to embroider infinite folk-lore from all ages and nations. Turner's sunlit picture flings over it a radiance that almost transfigures the horrible romance. Diana's priest, the " King of the Woods," armed with his drawn sword, lurks to this day among the enchanted trees above the Lake of Nemi—

> Those trees in whose dim shadow
> The ghastly priest doth reign,
> The priest who slew the slayer
> And shall himself be slain.

Renan, who had often passed by it, described the Lake and its fringe of sylvan foliage, as the " most amazing bit of fairy-land " he had ever seen. Priest, therefore, has slain priest time out of mind, succeeding by this awful rite to the Arician sanctuary. Thus far Ovid, Statius, the Latin historians. Now comes our modern with his lesson for the age. Antistius ought to have murdered Tetricus; but he spared that ruffian, who died of grief, and was himself elected priest by a popular vote. He puts down human sacrifice, converts the oracle to a pulpit, teaches the Sibyl Carmenta his doctrine of light and purity, declines to make a gain by imposture, and foretells the greatness of Rome. It follows that he is hated of his mother-city, Alba Longa. The people call him atheist; the soldiers charge upon him their own defeats. Ganeo, profligate and coward, expresses public opinion in one way, Metius, the aristocrat, in another; but they agree that Antistius ought to be removed. In the end Casca slays him; the old ritual of blood is set up once more, and order reigns in Alba Longa. Yet Carmenta prophesies in a frenzied strain that Rome will triumph. For Alba Longa read France, for Rome Germany, and draw the conclusion.

But Antistius, the Liberal, what good has he done his country by preaching the truth, nay, by suffering martyrdom in behalf of it? Has he not been righteous overmuch? " Yes," he cries, " a truth benefits only the soul that discovers it; one man's meat is another man's poison. Ah, be thou accursed, light which I have loved! Thou hast betrayed me. I was eager to reform the race of men; I have led them astray. O joy of life, thou spring of greatness and affection, to these wretches thou art become the source of all that is degrading! "

Here it will be worth while to quote M. Bourget, who for years was Renan's close follower.

Akin to him in sensitive refinement, in a certain
elegance bordering on effeminacy, and in the culture of exotic literature, he deserved to wear Eli-
jah's mantle. But M. Bourget it is who asks
whether in the moral agony of this revolutionary
priest we ought not to recognize the master's act
of contrition.

"In painting the Christ as he saw Him," observes the gentle critic, "he has helped to draw
away from the Church numbers who understood
in his books simply their negations. In giving
himself up to the pleasing reveries of a philosophic
fancy, he has spread abroad the latest of social
diseases; I mean, that dilettantism which combines
with rarest gifts of intellect a paralysis of the will.
Assuredly, he did not intend his works to have
these consequences. But he cannot deny them.
How, then, should he not ask himself whether the
things he has handled did not deserve to be respected, even at the cost of his own silence?"

Renan has anticipated the question, as is clear
from the drama; but while he resolves it in one
way when the priest of Nemi speaks he gives another and an opposite solution when he speaks
himself. For he is always the oracle which we
may interpret as we please. "No," he exclaims
in the preface, "I have not been among the timid
who believe that truth needs a penumbra." He

almost contradicts a wise old French proverb when he goes on to tell us, " Toute vérité est bonne à savoir." And, as we saw not many lines previously, he has put the exact reverse of this affirmation into the mouth of Antistius. Moreover, rejoins M. Bourget, is every passing opinion, be it called science or history, a truth? Is it not, in Renan's own words, one thing to opine, another to be certain? If a man struggling toward the light is edifying to all who mark his heroic efforts, what could be more dangerous than the self-indulgent mood which comes to no conclusion? Against that form of Nihilism, even because it caresses and beguiles, M. Bourget lifts a warning voice. But he would fain perceive in Antistius the martyr whose blood is the seed of victory, rather than a disheartened and despairing reformer.

M. Séailles is not so lenient. By choice of names and force of contrast, he declares, *The Priest of Nemi* announces that French civilization will be swept away in a Teutonic flood. Renan, he truly says, hated war; his counsels, however bravely meant, implied surrender. All had been flung into the melting-pot—property, patriotism, religion, family life, in Alba Longa, while Rome was building up a new society and writing its immortal Code. Antistius, by the lips of Carmenta, pleads for those Germans who in the nineteenth century had every kind of wisdom, against the elegant but corrupt French who had none. Thus far M. Séailles, the most independent of critics.

A parallel may here be suggested which often recurs to the mind as we turn over Renan's correspondence. The singular, nay, the unique and baffling element in all he writes, is that every thought calls out its contrary. Feeling on this side, reason on that, hold a dialogue which comes to no reconcilement, for want of common terms between the persons of the drama. Obedient to reason, cold and neutral, this man had forsaken his Church and stripped the Redeemer of divine attributes; but still he worshipped Jesus, he felt the charm of Apostolic Rome. Once more *The Priest of Nemi* exhibits him as divided between his mother-country—"la belle pécheresse," in the strong figure which some one has employed—and the German conqueror, whose weapon, like that of Achilles, heals where it wounds. Again he loves, but loses heart, gives up what is dear to him, yet lingers by the death-bed which he cannot console.

He had done his utmost. France needed a reformation in its governing ideas. "Woe to that generation," he had told his countrymen before the evil days fell upon them, "which takes life to be idle rest and the arts to be mere enjoyment!" But his own courage was failing. "Let us neither affirm nor deny," he said with a helpless gesture, as of one sinking into an opium-dream. Yet he added, "An immense moral debasement, nay, perhaps an intellectual one, will set in as soon as religion disappears." By way of enforcing this salutary lesson, he put his hand to a work which Madame Darmesteter, his enthusiastic friend, calls "an aberration of the moral instinct," and which lowered him in the eyes of Matthew Arnold, whose theological writings echo more than one of Renan's principles, but do not sacrifice to "the great goddess Lubricity."

The *Abbess of Jouarre* is offered to readers who welcome Platonic myths in modern French. It is not an edifying story. The nun who breaks her vow in presence of death, when condemned to the guillotine by revolutionary France, is not only grotesque, but ignoble; her accomplice, D'Arcy, is an odious and cold-blooded reasoner, of the worst eighteenth century type; and if, as M. Séailles insists, they are both pupils of Renan, we pity the schoolmaster. But the moral of this performance is even more astonishing than its execution. "I often imagine," says the author placidly, "that if mankind knew for certain the world would come to an end in two or three days, love "—he calls it love—" would break out on all sides with a sort of frenzy; for that which restrains love is the limit put upon it by the need of keeping society intact." These universal Saturnalia would be " high adoration " and " perfect prayer," comparable to the ecstasies of primitive Christians.

Perhaps Mr. Arnold's comment on the spirit which dictated so peculiarly Gallic a rendering of the Last Day will suffice here. It was written before the *Abbess* had come on the boards, which makes it, if possible, more apposite. " Even though a gifted man like M. Renan," he observed in his *American Lectures* of 1883, " may be so carried away by the tide of opinion in France where he lives, as to say that Nature cares nothing about chastity, and to see with amused indulgence the worship of the great goddess Lubricity, let us stand fast and say that her worship is against nature—human nature—and that it is ruin." He drives the lesson home in words equally to our purpose : " The Eternal has attached to certain moral causes the safety or ruin of States, and the present popular literature of France is a sign that she has a most dangerous moral disease."

This, too, is the witness of M. Taine, whose candid studies led him to conclude that Christian virtues are the wings which bear up civilized society. " Ever and always," he affirms in a wellknown passage, " for eighteen hundred years, so soon as those wings droop or are broken, public and private morals decline. In Italy during the Renaissance, in England under the Restoration, in France under the Convention and the Directory, we see men turn Pagans as in the first century of our era. By the same token they became what they were in the days of Augustus and Tiberius, voluptuous and hard. They misused others and themselves. Selfishness, brutal or cunning, had got the upper hand. Cruelty and sensuality flaunted their colors, and society was converted into a den of thieves or a house of shame."

Certainly, it may be rejoined, but the *Abbess* denies none of these things. To which we answer that, if the *Abbess* means what Renan had always in view—not an imagined Last Day, but " France where he lived "—his play condones decadent morals and sets the future on a hazard. " The century in which I have passed my time," he said when summing up his recollections, " will probably not turn out to be the greatest, but surely it will be reckoned the most amusing of ages." And elsewhere he judges a period of national decline to be the pleasantest for men like himself.

Not, then, shame or repentance, but a plenary indulgence, of which no good works were a condition—to accept one's disease and enjoy it—is the supreme duty, as we learn it from the *Abbess of*

Jouarre. The pride of science, which had at one time inspired him with a vision of the last wise man, still reasoning amid the shock of worlds, has given place to a sensual curiosity. There is no longer an aim in life or knowledge. Carried away by the flood of phenomena, Renan loses in his work its ideal unity, in his busy days any definite scope; he wanders more and more astray from the goal which he had set himself at starting. " Dulcia vitia ! " he would tell us in the words he addressed to Jules Sandeau. But is it not rather the breaking up of a great intellectual empire into rebel provinces, where the desert invades and ancient cities fall to ruin? We cannot but see in all this the dissolution of a soul which was originally destined to enlighten the world.

His last undertaking, the *History of Israel,* was completed before he died, but only in part revised. These five volumes need not detain us long. Style and thought could not be wanting to them; passages of rare subtlety call up the enchanter we have known; but he comes after men like Ewald, who were deeply religious and inherited something of the prophetic spirit; or like Kuenen and Wellhausen, original explorers, in whose light his literary displays grow dim. For half a century he had been occupied with Hebrew lore; his attention had been drawn to the possible results in that province of epigraphy; but he discovered little and suggested nothing new.

Moreover, while he followed the latest of the *chorizontes,* who broke up the sacred text until it showed as many colors as the rainbow wherever one opened it, a conservative reaction was approaching. The monuments were building up what the philologists had pulled down. Babylon was already furnishing a commentary upon Genesis which earlier sceptics had never dreamed of, and which their descendants could not resist. The amazing revelations of Tel el Amarna were soon to transform our whole view of Assyrian and Egyptian relations at a highly significant period for believers in Scripture. Archæology, in the words of Professor Sayce, was tending to " substantiate the historical trustworthiness of the older records of the Hebrew people and the antiquity of the documents which contain them." *A priori* conjectures, ingenious emendations of the text, " all carved out of the carver's brain," must give way to actual and contemporary evidence. It had become more entertaining to read Lenormant, Brugsch, Pinches, Schrader, and their fellow-workers, than to listen while a fatigued man of letters polished up his favorite sarcasms, handled David somewhat in the manner of Voltaire, and betrayed his want of acquaintance with primitive folk-lore.

In spite of his Oriental learning, his travels in the East, and his boundless curiosity, we feel something in Renan which will not let him enter, as deeply as his subject requires, into that ancient world. He is too Greek or too French. Imperfect sympathy creates a barrier between this dainty, over-refined Western and the rude greatness of the Biblical heroes. All that he could tell us about his own thoughts, hinted in eloquent paragraphs, will not serve instead of the power which he was unable to wield. When he comes down to the age before Christianity, and Alexandria becomes the meeting-place of Hebrew and Hellene, as in Philo, his magic staff recovers its virtue. But the Israel of the Old Testament, for which he always cherished an aversion, did not inspire him. The Prophets themselves were " violent tribunes of justice "; and their visions of the supernatural could be to him only the baseless fabric of a dream.

Thus he was drawing near the end, never idle, calm and cheery, much loved, flattered, and even spoiled by an indulgent France. After his *Reminiscences* came out, he went down in August, 1884, to Tréguier, on which he had not set eyes during some forty years. The Bretons are fervent Catholics; but they were willing to see in this unfrocked seminarist a man of their race and language whom

the great world adored. He made up his mind
to live among them; and at Rosmapamon discovered the house, " parva sed apta mihi," as he told
Berthelot, smiling, which became his summer re-
sort onward from 1885. He planned a new journey to the East. But he never went thither again.
His grandchildren were a joy and entertainment
to the scholar, who had always been something
of a child himself. He presided at Breton dinners, lifted his glass in homage to Béranger, rebuked the growing sadness of youth, and taught
the philosophy of Hedonism.

We read in St. Paul that there are many graces,
but one spirit who gives them. Renan parodies
the sacred words. " The means of salvation," he
writes in his *Loose Leaves* (the English title fits
them on this occasion), " are not the same for all.
To one, virtue is the means; to another, pursuit of
truth; to another, art; to yet others, curiosity,
ambition, travel, luxury, the fair sex, riches; on
the lowest grade morphine and alcohol. The
most dangerous mistake, as regards the morals of
human society, is to put down pleasure on system."

His own pleasure, if not sanctified by the high
mark at which he had ceased to aim, was in its
kind not ignoble. As administrator in the Collège
de France he did his duty; and he continued his
lectures in spite of illness, until he had almost to

be carried into his chair. The rooms assigned him were narrow and uncomfortable. " I have had a good deal to put up with," he wrote in a private memorandum found among his papers, " sometimes even downright poverty, but never, never was I so wretchedly lodged as in the Collège de France." He made no public complaint. Berthelot and Renan looked with disquietude on incidents like the adventure of Boulanger; the debasement of France was setting in more strongly than ever. " Our incurable *étourderie,* our want of organization, our illusions, frighten me," said Renan to his friend in 1888; " but we are old. The just measure of life has been vouchsafed us; we have had our five acts; we should be unfair did we protest too much. It is not an ill condition, nor does it lack a certain charm, to behave as a dying man, *moriturus.*"

The last long expedition which he undertook was to the Riviera toward the end of 1891. He was always correcting the proofs of his *Israel,* fearing if another did it by and by that he should suffer more on that account in purgatory. His rheumatic pains never left him. In July, 1892, he was at Rosmapamon, whence his last letter to the friend of his youth is dated. " How well we did," he writes, " to choose our philosophy of life when we were young and strong! How late it

would be to think of these things when the end
threatens and we must expect a removal! All that
is not new to me. To end is nothing; I have almost fulfilled by life's plan; I could make good
use of some years yet; but I am ready to go. It
is hard, I grant, that one should be the cause of
grief to others, and should trouble the lives of
those who are dear to one. In that matter, a reasonable *euthanasia,* guided by sound philosophy,
could do much."

In his *Reminiscences* he had provided against
what he considered the accidents whereby Augustin Thierry and Littré had given the lie to their
former opinions. " I protest in advance," he declared, " against the foolish things (*les faiblesses*)
which softening of the brain might lead me to say
or to subscribe. It is Renan whole in mind and
heart, as I am this day, not Renan half the prey
of death, as I shall be if I am slowly to break up,
for whom I desire credit and attention. I abjure
the blasphemies which one last hour of weakness
might elicit from me against the Eternal."

He was not to be tempted. A sudden failure
of the heart warned him that his days were num-
bered. " Take me back to the College," he insisted; and his devoted wife obeyed. There,
among friends and kinsfolk, he died without suffering on October 2, 1892. " That great intel-

lect," says the *Livre d'Or,* compiled by his admirers, " which had reflected so many aspects of human thought, expired in peace and in absolute negation."

The French Republic, though he had never loved it, gave him a State funeral. Before his coffin, M. Bourgeois, Minister of Education, and many others, held orations in the College vestibule. Senators, deputies, generals, judges, delegates from learned societies, officials of every rank, students, professors, diplomatists, all came flocking to do him honor. The Grand Orient of France sent a wreath for his coffin, which was hidden by the floral crowns cast upon it. During its passage to the grave a detachment of infantry accompanied its march, thousands of spectators lined the streets. It had been proposed that Renan should find a resting-place under the dome of the Pantheon, formerly Ste. Geneviève, which was secularized to make room for the relics of Victor Hugo not many years previously. But difficulties arose, and the body was committed, by Madame Renan's wish, to the vault of her own family, the Scheffers, at Montmartre. His wife survived him less than two years, dying on May 22, 1894; his son Ary, who was winning distinction as a poet and a draughtsman, and who seems to have been of a very amiable character, died on August 4, 1900. Madame Psichari, Renan's daughter, lives with her children in the country house of Rosmapamon.

By anticipation the man himself sketched his own epitaph, not on the walls of a cemetery, but, as was fitting, during a banquet at Tréguier, when he first went back thither in 1884. It is Renan's *Apologia pro Vita Suâ,* which in justice ought not to be passed over. "I should like," he said, "to have written on my tomb—ah, if it could be in the midst of that cloister, but the cloister is the Church, and the Church, mistakenly enough, will have nothing to do with me—but I wish to have on my tomb these words, *Veritatem dilexi.* Yes, I have loved the truth, sought it, followed whither it called me, without regard to the sacrifice entailed. I broke the links that were dearest to me that I might obey it. And I am sure that I did right. Let me express my meaning. No one can be certain that he understands the riddle of the universe; the infinite that clasps us round escapes from all the lines and formulas we set upon it. But one thing there is that we may affirm: sincerity of heart, devotion to truth, the consciousness of what we have given up for its sake. That witness I will hold, high and firm, above my head on the Day of Judgment."

Who could find it in his heart to gainsay these passionate words, or to question whether Renan believed what he uttered so resolutely? But the Latin proverb warns us, "Exitus acta probat," and a tree is known by its fruits. M. Séailles, contemplating the teacher's whole course, affirms that he "mistook indecision for sincerity"; that when he quitted St. Sulpice it was not only the enthusiasm of a truth-seeker which moved him, but terror lest he should be committed beyond recall by advancing to the priesthood; and that his love of "the Truth" ended in a defeat which had nothing to boast of but its resignation.

Another has observed, in view of the philosopher's last achievements, intended to win applause from an unreformed world, "saltavit et placuit," he danced to a music which his better sense condemned as lascivious and obscene. In a gentler mood Alphonse Daudet likened him to a cathedral which has been desecrated to profane uses, but where amid the hay, straw, and stubble, while the choir is turned to a messroom, and the stalls are a stabling for horses, it is impossible to forget that the building was once a church. And yet another saying, uttered in fierce wrath by Ludovicus Vives against the Arabian sceptic, Averroes, may be applied to this versatile teacher, "He must needs grow impious and atheistical who is vehemently given to the study of thy writings." Such, at all events, was the opinion held by those French pub-

The Statue of Ernest Renan at Trêguier.

lic men who saw in his State funeral a protest
against all religion and against the Christian in
particular.

How now, we may further ask, will the epitaph
look which we have cited above, when set in a
parallel column with another passage equally authentic? "We stake our nobility," says Renan,
with pride, "on an obstinate affirmation of duty.
But," he continues, "there are almost as many
chances that the opposite may be true. It may be
that these voices within us are the consequence of
sincere delusions, kept up by habit, and that the
world is an amusing transfiguration-scene which no
god has in his care. We must then so arrange
as on either supposition not to be entirely in the
wrong. We ought to mind those higher voices,
but in such a way that if the second hypothesis
turns out to be a fact, we shall not have been altogether duped." Here is the clean contrary of
what was said at Tréguier. But we may write on
the same page even a third quotation, no less genuine: "Religion, which sums up man's ethical needs
—virtue, modesty, disinterestedness, and self-sac-
rifice—is the voice of the universe."

Astonishing vitality, boundless incoherence, these
were Renan's qualities and defects. Nature had
refused him the graces; but his "leonine" head,
his features marked with a penetrating intelligence,

his eyes lighting up under slow eyelids, could never have suited with a common man. His voice had many tones in it, strong, flexible, caressing, always, however, self-controlled. His robust and healthy make, his temperance, and his very studies, which for years led him into libraries rather than where men debated for their lives, or artists hung feverishly over their canvas, brought him past the age of temptation. All this gave him power and inclination to attempt the chief enterprise by which he is known; it saved him when old and somewhat frivolously minded from pitfalls in which other literary heroes had lost their character. At all the turning-points in life he showed energy as well as decision. Except from his sister Henriette he seems never to have asked advice. Early and late he took his own way. He acknowledged in Augustin Thierry a " spiritual master "; but he was not familiar with Thierry when he changed his course in 1845. Intellectual ancestors he had none outside books; and if disciples came, he did not seek them.

His place in French literature is a lonely one, more than Balzac's or even Flaubert's. And his manner of speech is inimitable. M. Bourget tells a pleasant story of the critic who could analyze every great style and lay bare its secret; when the talk fell on Renan, he shook his head. " Ah, that man's phrase," he exclaimed; "one sees not how it is made." In fact, it was not made. Touches, no doubt, of infinite delicacy brought out the required expression. The master was never weary of correcting himself. His manuscripts abound in erasures; his printed revisions went on for months. But the character of his phrase may be ascribed to a vitality which fostered the inward sense, to exercise in the logic of the Schools, to much reading in classical authors, and to the self-denial which would not allow his pen easily to run after Chateaubriand or Hugo, landscape-painters whom he could not rival and would not stoop to imitate. His richness, or depth of allusion, an uncommon quality among French writers, was no trick. It was the spontaneous pouring out of knowledge; the discovery of new horizons consequent on his travels through the learned world, which men of letters in Paris did not explore. To unite culture with science, erudition with life and poetry, views the most diverse with a temperament which had always been "gay yet resigned," was to create a genius entirely novel, and the corresponding expression could not but follow in due season.

Renan maintained that he had no need to use any words except those which he found in the seventeenth century. Gautier and St. Victor replied that the ideas which he uttered in them flung over those words a modern air and seeming. His critics were surely in the right. Nevertheless, one reason why he charms and subdues so many, is the dressing up in perfect but unpretending French of thoughts which are bold to the point of revolution. Anarchic, subtle, perverse, dissolving as a poison they may prove to be; but they are always elegantly attired, and as insinuating as music which lulls to sleep on a much loved rhythm. To this effect his citations from the Latin Vulgate, his fondness for devotional terms, his pretty " peal of church bells," as he calls it himself, added extraordinary power. Never was a certain verse of Shakespeare about quoting Scripture for a purpose more strikingly illustrated.

By such handling the sacred became all the more profane; Holy Writ was made its own refutation; and Judas betrayed his Master with a kiss. To smile was deadlier in its office than to sneer. Sympathy turned out to be the sharpest criticism. But how irresistible its advances! For who could be deaf to the voice of this charmer? He did not argue or contend; he suggested, like faint echoes among the hills, your own thoughts to you, until they died away in a tingling silence. But something was gone out of them, and you could not believe any more. Whatever delights us in Renan comes from the past with which he had broken.

All the secret bitterness, and despair in the end, he has added from his own stores. He is a magician who reverses the rod of power when illusion is at its height. That disenchantment he terms philosophy; the reversed rod is modern science; and for the divine Prospero we must put up with Caliban, who will, perhaps, not rend us in pieces until the drunken fit seizes him once more.

If a better interpretation of Renan's wisdom can be found, it shall be welcome. Meanwhile, history has provided a contrast. The man who shared with him an influence over the rising French generation as great as Stuart Mill's had been in England between 1860 and 1880, was Hippolyte Taine. Pupil and professor of the Normal School, Taine had renounced his Christian parentage, given to Hegel a literary form and pressure which made him a prophet side by side with Rousseau in a land not his own, and declared thought to be a secretion of the brain, free will a figment, our most certain experience a " fixed hallucination." If not atheist or materialist by force of terms, he was both in the popular judgment. Assuredly, no writer in the *Journal des Débats* carried more weight; none was a greater enemy of the " clerical " opposition. Yet, in mid-course, Taine, and not another, undertaking from documents and evidence to deal with the French Revolution on its merits, saw himself obliged, as a candid historian, to condemn it more severely than Carlyle had ever done; nay, to repeat in sentences crowded with facts undeniable the language of Edmund Burke.

Taine went a step farther. In the Christian creed and ceremonies; in its catechism and its ideals; this determined agnostic, as for thirty years he had appeared in all his writings, now perceived the source of French greatness. The religious idea, the stay and foundation of society during fifteen hundred years, had been annihilated by Jacobins, who vainly strove to put in its place their lay education, lay church, lay ethics. But all they had accomplished was to ruin the ancient buildings, after which they took refuge in Napoleon's barracks. For his own part, Taine, though he did not become a Catholic, found in Christian teaching the only hope, and submitted his once recalcitrant spirit to its guidance. He cast from him the Revolution in every shape, whether as unbelieving science, militant atheism, or State monopoly; but he did so in the name of unanswerable witnesses—the dead who had spoken by their acts and monuments which every one could examine for himself.

The six volumes that describe the *Origins of Contemporary France* were at once an indictment and a censure. They were received with shouts of amazement, then with silence; but they never have been refuted. In this "terrible book" we may study the consequences of a philosophic system which Renan, despite his ingenuities and ironies, could not escape from. He was no Jacobin, politically speaking; but Robespierre and his acolytes carried into execution the ideas that everywhere lie hidden beneath Renan's graceful persiflage. He, too, had indicted the new order of things, almost as decidedly as the historian now did; but he had yielded to its sway because, after all, what in him was a timid and refined sentiment, starting back from its own shadow, in the Convention had become a deadly logic, armed with sword and axe for the destruction of its foes.

A benevolent critic, M. Lanson, tells us that Renan has "for many minds rendered faith impossible, and equally impossible the war against faith"; he has made an end of the Voltairian spirit, says M. Lanson, and delivered those who cannot be Christians from being anti-clerical. "Neither believers nor enemies, nay rather sympathizers with belief, conscious that faith is morally good for those who can hold by it, such is what Renan has made of us." Taine will prove to the observant reader how empty, if how amiable, is that delusion. In the world of which we form part, indifference to a creed is hostility so victorious, that it does not know the grave in which its conquered enemy lies buried. Renan was in religion what the Gironde was in French politics, flowery, inconsequent, the slave dragged behind a triumphal chariot which he had helped to set in motion. His *Life of Jesus* may be summed up in the famous expression of Vergniaud, presiding at the trial of Louis XVI: " I regret to declare that by a majority of votes Louis Capet has been judged worthy of death." It is the headsman's eloquence, while Christianity lies bound on the scaffold, waiting until the axe shall fall.

In everything the confirmed dilettante is a prey to his own dramatic fancies; the real, the lasting abides far from him. Of religion, philosophy, love, heroism, he may counterfeit the semblance; but he can boast no more. He is Ixion enamored of a cloud. He plays a part on the stage; woe to the charmed spectator who mistakes it for something real. In Ernest Renan the reality was a wide and curious erudition, hung round with shining jewels from all possible systems; but the jewels were paste. His creed may be brought down to a single negation, " The supernatural does not exist." When we inquire of the oracle, " What, then, shall we do to possess everlasting life? " he answers, " Do as seems right in your own eyes." All differences are swallowed up in the gulf of a fundamental unity. Nero and Paul, Judas and

Jesus, are chords in one great orchestra. How, indeed, should it be otherwise when we have reduced the personalities, which make men each to be himself and incommunicable, to scientific expressions with a common measure?

The whole tangled web of Renan's contradictions unfolds itself when we follow this clue. He brings us down to the abstract, impersonal element which in Hegel, or Averroes, or Spinoza is the One Everlasting. And our universe of spirits or monads is borne along the stream of tendency, always passive, though not always inobservant. A wise man will often smile at the turn which things are taking, but he never resists. Why should he? The intellect is one thing, the will another; and except for the will how can there be a difference between good and evil? To the philosophic mind all phenomena which it can perceive must be agreeable, since all are equally objects of its contemplation.

Here, then, we reach our last analysis. Life, art, religion, divorced from will, distilled into atomic formulas, have had taken out of them spontaneity, the free personal initiative—that which in morals is virtue, in thought judgment, in enterprise faith, in act resolution. The attempt to view all things as if the mind which views them did not count, is intellectual suicide. One-half of our nature, and that the more important, is thereby suppressed. The real unity, to which every man refers as to a centre all his doings, is sacrificed to a fictitious *caput mortuum* called science, where its faculties lose their meaning and are no longer recognizable. In that unity, secret and deep as life itself, the primal truths spring up which, on entering into contact with experience, make us sure of our own existence as self-conscious beings, of the world outside us, and of the laws under which we are bound to live.

Will it be said that there are no such laws? But if that be inconceivable, and if science, as defined by Renan, cannot discover them, what is the inference? Surely that "science," handled upon this method, is inadequate and misleading. Though it should break down, the problem of duty remains as imperious as ever, and therefore cannot be insoluble. Another method, a calculus of the spirit, must be applied; or we shall judge like the man born blind that colors do not exist, like the untaught savage that letters have no meaning. Renan's enormous negative which, in denying the supernatural, swept away all that we live by— God, conscience and immortality—sets, therefore, the seal on his incompetence as a great teacher. Why incompetent? Because he had taken as ultimate criteria of the truth physics masquerading in the shape of history, sentiment for first principles, imagination for judgment, and a dead, or half-dead stream of tendency, for the Love which a greater than he has celebrated:

That moves the sun in heaven and all the stars.

Remarkable as was Taine's conversion from that unsound philosophy, and decisive the proofs which he brought against it, considered in the light of an experiment lasting now more than a hundred years, while France was dying in the moral vacuum it had created, a yet more complete overthrow was inflicted upon it by one before whom Taine veils his crest as a thinker—we mean, of course, Cardinal Newman. Singularly impressive is the contrast, in every stage conspicuous, between the Oxford divine and the Parisian dilettante. Agreeing as they did in their conception of literature, in devotion to Greek and Roman antiquity, in disdain of the applause which is caught by picturesque language, in their superb isolation from the crowd, and in their gifts of irony and brilliant humor, they set out from contradictory premises to arrive at opposite conclusions.

Newman is a Mystic, Renan a Rationalist. To Newman his conscience makes known a present Deity; but to Renan it is a human invention without echo in the heights or the depths. The one enlarges on the " ventures of faith "; by the other we are warned not to be the dupes of our better feelings. Prayer is the philosophy on which Newman feeds his mind; to Renan prayer has become absurd, for what is it more than talking to one's self? Reverence, adoration, shame and holy fear betoken that the one is face to face with a Supreme Judge, in whose kindness he revives, under whose frown he wastes away. The other sees no intellect superior to his own; reveres no divinity; suppresses the idea of sin; loses the delicacy of feeling which protects all exquisite virtue; and writes his page in the scandalous chronicle of French letters. With Newman, learning, style, eloquence, are but means to a nobler end; he is always intent on religion, even where he comes down to a schoolmaster's exercises. But Renan, who began at the same starting-point, turns all this another way. The lowest knowledge is the only real truth; art loses its former interest; religion is a pretty make-believe, ethics a lottery, life itself an entertainment. Thus, to the meditative Newman things eternal grow more and more vivid; as he realizes the Divine Attributes, man takes on him grander proportions, becomes the heir of infinite hopes, and is called to heroic deeds. This golden key of personality unlocks doors which remain obstinately barred when the Parisian science beats upon them.

In such a way is absolute negation met by no less resolute assertion. But the denials that scatter Renan's philosophy to the four winds, leaving him the wreck of his own fancies, cannot have much to commend them, since all his wonderful endowments do not avail to save him from incoherence and despair. In one word, Newman has found Jesus; Renan has lost Him.

Such was the experiment, such the outcome of two lives, rich in their powers and opportunities, that, filling the nineteenth century with their fame, have left to after ages a picture of themselves, and bear on to a future day the undying strife between light and darkness. How much of either will survive? We cannot tell. But not on arts of literature, equal in both, will the issue depend. If men turn sceptics; if society cultivates decadence as a pastime; if the bands of Orion are loosened, and Pagan ethics drive out Christian from the bridal-chamber, the schools, the printing-press, to say nothing of the market and the exchange, to this movement of dissolution Renan will have lent a powerful hand. For by denial or by surrender he has made these things possible.

Should, however, a creative breath renew the world, and man become once more the being of transcendent worth which he thought himself at all heroic eras, not much will be left of Renan except his memory as an artist, and specimens, carefully chosen from forbidden volumes, to illustrate that marvellous gift. The incalculable quality which, for want of a better name, we call genius, and which is, at last, personality carried to its highest power, will never be denied him. As a master of his native tongue, limpid, unforced, enchanting, whose only fault was even too great a dexterity, the Breton remains worthy of a place beside Chateaubriand, over against Lamennais, inspired by the charm of that French idiom which in those eloquent preachers sounded tragic and sombre, but from his pen flowed in a smiling stream. In history, little that he attempted will be remembered. As a thinker he does not count. Who would name Renan amid the senate of philosophers, German or Greek? But he had something of that which, in his forerunner, Abelard, cast over the man of letters, the Parisian professor, the classic yet romantic medieval doctor, a gleam of imperishable renown. Abelard opened the way to an alliance between the Church and Aristotle by his very aberrations; Renan stated, though he could not resolve, the problem of Scripture-criticism. From the day when his *Life of Jesus* appeared the Bible has become for clergy no less than laity a modern book, the most momentous in living literature.

On August 30, 1902, the town council of Tréguier voted, by a majority of eleven to five, that a monument should be erected to Renan in one of its public squares. A committee was formed, including, besides French celebrities, foreign names like George Meredith, Ibsen, Maeterlinck, Galdos, Brandes, Gerard Hauptmann, and Mommsen. The bronze seated figure, above which rises Athena to signify the ideal which he worshipped, is now in its place. But, by way of protest, the Catholic Bretons have set up an image of Calvary over against it. "To give Renan a monument," said M. Anatole France, "is to erect one to science and wisdom." Renan himself has written, "A beautiful work is that which represents, under finite and individual traits, the infinite, the everlasting beauty of human nature." He said also, "Error founds nothing; no error can last very long." By those sentences let him be judged.

In the *Suppliants* of Euripides, three lines occur which a believer may well apply to the French iconoclast—

> Ἀλλ' ἡ φρόνησις τοῦ θεοῦ μεῖζον σθένειν
> ζητεῖ, τὸ γαῦρον δ'ἐν φρεσὶν κεκτημένοι
> δοκοῦμεν εἶναι δαιμόνων σοφώτεροι.

A sentiment of which the drift would perhaps be expressed in English as follows—

Our thought presumes to scan the mind of God
And finds it wanting; thus, with pride possessed,
Wiser than angels we esteem ourselves.

That epitaph, inscribed on Ernest Renan's tomb, would shadow forth a mind which, looking out into the universe, saw nothing to worship but its own powers, and which ended in absolute negation. The faith it had given up held for others the light of life; but in the knowledge to which it aspired it found only darkness visible.

THE END

LITERARY LIVES

Edited by ROBERTSON NICOLL, D. D.

Each volume illustrated, $1.00 net. (Postage, 10 cents.)

THIS series is intended to furnish biographical and critical studies of well-known authors of all countries. Distinguished writers, British and American, contribute to it. While much freedom has been allowed the contributors, it will be found that the special aim of supplying full critical and expository estimates has been kept steadily in view. In many cases additions have been made to the store of existing information, and the books should take a place, not only for their biographical value, but as helpful companions and interpreters in the study of literary masterpieces.

CHARLES SCRIBNER'S SONS NEW YORK

LITERARY LIVES

'Each volume illustrated, $1.00 net.   (Postage, 10 cents.)

NEW VOLUMES

ERNEST RENAN
By WILLIAM BARRY, D.D.

CONTENTS

An account of the life and work of a scholar and author written seriously yet pleasantly and full of the charm and brilliancy of the extraordinary man of whom it gives so interesting and vivid a portrait.

CHARLOTTE BRONTË
By CLEMENT K. SHORTER

Mr. Shorter, the author of this new life of the most famous of the Brontës, is already widely known as the writer of many discriminating and suggestive essays in literature and biography. It would have been difficult to find a more sympathetic or appropriate author for this new volume of the "Literary Lives."

CHARLES SCRIBNER'S SONS   NEW YORK

LITERARY LIVES

Each volume illustrated, $1.00 net. (Postage, 10 cents).

COVENTRY PATMORE

By EDMUND GOSSE

CONTENTS

Early Years (1823-1846)
Life in London (1846-1862)
Hampstead and Heron's Ghyll
  (1862-1870)

"The Angel in the House"
Last Years (1870-1896)
Personal Characteristics
Literary Position and Aims

" A well-balanced and interesting biography . . . . a careful, sympathetic, but entirely clear-sighted estimate of Patmore's poetic gifts and of the value of his work."—*The Outlook.*

Mr. Gosse has made a delightful little book about Patmore. Even to those to whom Patmore has been a name and a name only, it will be delightful."—*New York Times Review.*

JOHN BUNYAN

By W. HALE WHITE

CONTENTS

The Life and "Grace Abounding"
The Preacher
"The Pilgrim's Progress"
The "Holy War"

The "Life and Death of
  Mr. Badman"
Some Reflections on Bunyan
  and Puritanism

" No more perfect biographer could have been found for Bunyan. There is something Puritanical in the exquisite simplicity of his style, his high seriousness, his keen sympathy, which is saved from partisanship by the breadth and philosophy of his outlook."—*London Spectator.*

"Mr. White's book . . . will be found interesting and helpful to an understanding of the genius and inspiration of the author of 'The Pilgrim's Progress.' "—*Brooklyn Eagle.*

CHARLES SCRIBNER'S SONS   NEW YORK

LITERARY LIVES

Each volume illustrated, $1.00 net.   (Postage, 10 cents.)

MATTHEW ARNOLD
By G. W. E. RUSSELL

CONTENTS

Introduction
Method
Education

Society
Conduct
Theology

"We get from this book a vivid personal impression of benefits received from association with his ideas. . . . It is not only an interesting but a valuable contribution to the literature already gathered about its subject."—*New York Times.*

"Mr. Russell's book offers a concise, illuminating introduction to the systematic study of the works of the master of light and sweetness, and is good literature."—*Boston Herald.*

CARDINAL NEWMAN
By WILLIAM BARRY, D. D.

CONTENTS

Early Years
The Tractarians
First Catholic Period
Apologia pro Vita Sua

The Logic of Belief
Dream of Gerontius
The Man of Letters
Newman's Place in History

"A surprising book that will arouse thought and discussion, and which will stand by its literary quality. Interesting from cover to cover, and written in English that Newman himself would not disown."—*New York Sun.*

"A book to be read with keen interest by all who have been attracted by one of the most fascinating and most baffling personalities of the nineteenth century."—*London Literary World.*

CHARLES SCRIBNER'S SONS   **NEW YORK**

morituris
laudaturus
laudandus